D0359805

ADVANCE PRAISE FOR

"Content Rich: Writing Your Way to Wealth on the Web"

www.ContentRichBook.com

"This is the most important business book you will read this year. Nothing will make a bigger impact on your sales than applying what you learn here. Jon is the best in the industry and that is why we rely on his advice. Google has changed all of the rules of business and this book will give you the new playbook."
—Roman Bodnarchuk, Chairman and CEO: www.N5R.com

"Companies have paid ad agencies $200K to tell them what they'll find in this book for $20. Jon Wuebben's information on growing your online presence could revolutionize sales for both small and large businesses alike. Buying this book is putting money in your pocket."
—Dianna Booher, Author – The Voice of Authority and E-Writing

"Filled with practical advice and insider secrets, Jon Wuebben gives business builders a master's class in using written content to increase search engine rankings, online traffic and sales. This useful jargon-free guide is filled with clear explanations, helpful examples and smart strategies. A terrific resource!"
—Lisa Johnson, Author - Mind Your X's and Y's:
Satisfying the Ten Cravings of a New Generation of Consumers

"Wow. I expected Jon's book to cover copywriting for the web, but it covers so much more than that. Its full of practical advice and specific examples – two things that are severely lacking in so many other "how to" guides for business on the web. Jon covers copywriting for the web, copy layout, on-page SEO, link building, conversion optimization, online PR and even gives advice and tips about running an internet-based service business. Jon's book is now mandatory reading for my new hires. Make sure to have your highlighter ready!"
— Jon Payne, Principal, Net Focus Media - www.netfocusmedia.com

"It is refreshing to see a concise book on the subject of copywriting with SEO in mind. Jon does a most excellent job defining the differences between traditional copywriting versus SEO copywriting. Whether a novice copywriter or seasoned veteran, this book will help one to understand how copywriting with SEO in mind can help improve not only organic search visibility but web site usability as well. I love how Jon explains in detail various types of SEO copywriting such as copywriting for articles, press releases, paid search ads, Wikis, email/newsletters, and even viral campaigns. I also enjoyed the real world examples of SEO copywriting for both small and large businesses. If you are in any way, shape or form involved with a web site, I highly recommend this book."

—David Wallace - Founder and CEO, SearchRank

"This book is essential reading for anyone serious about success online. A number of new mediums have appeared online which present both challenges and tremendous opportunities–these include blogs, RSS, and e-mail marketing, and this book does a fabulous job of explaining the nuances that must be mastered to achieve success in these new arenas. Want to learn the necessary steps for attracting and keeping website visitors? Content Rich is a must read…it is the most comprehensive book I know of that explains in thorough detail the steps necessary to write your way towards better search engine rankings and a tremendous increase in traffic to your site."

—David Chapman , Founder, Webrageous Studios

"Technology might change but the basic foundations of marketing stay the same. Simply put, you might have the greatest product in the world but if no one knows about it you aren't going to make any sales. So the key to any successful business is bringing in potential customers and making them clients.

Here's where Content Rich comes in. This book looks at ways to bring people to your website and how to encourage them to buy your product. To bring clients to your site, the author looks primarily at search engine optimization, making sure that your site rates well within Google, Yahoo, and other like search engines. The biggest concerns here are making sure that your metatag keywords and your actual site content work together for the best possible results.

Once you've got potential customers coming to your site, you can focus on making these people actual clients. Making sure your site is intuitive and easy to scan for the appropriate information is key. Adding a little buzz and regularly adding content will also help."

—TCM Reviews, www.tcm-ca.com

"The Internet has changed everything, including what works and what doesn't work in copywriting. If you want to stay competitive, you'll need to read Jon Wuebben's new book, Content Rich....several times."

—Al Ries, Co-Author, The Origin of Brands

"Whether you are in a business seeking to jumpstart sales or an established company that wants to increase search engine rankings, I would recommend Content Rich. The book not only discusses the importance of optimized copy, but breaks it down better than any other book on the topic. Content Rich is a great Web 2.0 resource and is the ultimate playbook for online copywriting."

—Adrian Gostick, New York Times bestselling author of The Carrot Principle

"Content Rich is full of the critical copywriting and search engine optimization information that you need to succeed online today. The increasing importance of SEO make this book a timely "must read" for e-business owners everywhere. In Content Rich, Jon Wuebben shares both his enthusiasm and the tactical specifics that you need to know to make your online business a success."

—Scott Fox, Author "Internet Riches", www.ScottFox.com

""No smoke and mirrors here…just sound advice for creating optimized content and improving your website's visibility in search engines – Content Rich is right on target"

—Greg Reilly, Partner, Rock Coast Media www.rockcoastmedia.com

"In this practical and idea-igniting book, Wuebben has delivered not only the fundamentals to success for SEO copywriting, but also the structure for delivering a sound and viable product to consumers online. His approaches to marketing a website to end consumers and the search engines are empowering and resounding. Wuebben shows, not tells, readers how to effectively build compelling online content with strong case studies from years of practical experience. Content Rich has enough food for thought to jumpstart the beginner online marketer as well as fine tune the practices of an industry veteran. If SEO or SEM is anywhere in your job description, this book is a must-read. It may also give the product team a run for their money as well!"

—Dena Yahya, General Manager – www.onetime.com

I see incredible value for whoever reads this book especially those looking to better understand how to not only write content for the edification of search engine visibility, but more importantly, write optimized content that converts it's end users into sales or desired actions when they arrive on-site!"
—Sean Bolton, Co-Founder & CEO, Lead To Conversion, LLC.

"It's not easy to make a book about writing copy to optimize your rankings on search engines (SEO) into a real page turner, but Jon Wuebben makes a valiant attempt.

For me, a novice in the field of web sales, the topic is just plain daunting, but that's my problem, not Wuebben's. The author uses simple, declarative sentences, a laidback conversational tone and plain English where he could be using "technobabble". His examples are straightforward, easy to follow and demonstrably convincing, even for the uninitiated. I found the apples-to-apples comparisons he uses very effective. By that I mean, he shows the copy as it looks before the improvements and SEO and then again after. The change was obvious, the explanations clear, and the result definitely beneficial. And, if I got it, so will everyone else.

My husband, with a Web history as old as the Web itself found it to be valuable as well. What impressed him most is that Wuebben cites other sources for his statistics, rather than simply personal research. This approach makes his assertions all the more compelling and gives real meat to his data. If you're looking to find a pot of gold over the Internet rainbow, Content Rich: Writing Your Way to Wealth on the Web may very well be your own ruby slippers. Armchair Interviews says: this is knowledge anyone who wants to generate traffic on the Web should know."
—www.Armchairinterviews.com

CONTENT
RICH

Writing Your Way to
Wealth on the Web

CONTENT
RICH

Writing Your Way to
Wealth on the Web

JON WUEBBEN

ENCORE
Publishing

A Telegent Media Company

Copyright © 2008 by Jon Wuebben

All rights reserved

Encore Publishing Group
124 S. Mercedes Road
Fallbrook, CA 92028

Visit our website at http://www.encorepublishers.com

Printed in the United States of America
First printing: April 2008

Cover design by Mike Fender
Interior book design by JustYourType.biz

Wuebben, Jon.

Content rich : writing your way to wealth on the Web

/ Jon Wuebben. — 1st ed.

p. cm.
Includes bibliographical references and index.

ISBN-13: 978-0-9797629-0-1

ISBN-10: 0-9797629-0-1

1. Web sites—Design. 2. Authorship. 3. Search
engines. I. Title.
TK5105.888.W84 2008 808'.066005

QBI08-600087

Table of Contents

Introduction

Words are powerful things. They help us communicate and help us connect. Spoken effectively, and they can build mighty empires or bring us closer to the ones we love. Words can impact society in new and different ways, help change perception or drive people to buy new products. Before the ink pen, printing press, typewriter and the Internet came along, the spoken word was king. It ruled the communication channel. And it did for centuries. Not anymore.

The written word has taken over. Its time has finally come.

How do we know? How about the 13 billion pages of written text on the Internet? Email is the communication of choice for most of us. CEO's of some major corporations don't even use the phone much anymore! Email is instant and efficient. It offers you the opportunity to think before hitting the send button and is something almost everyone seems to use. Some of us, especially those who have PDA's or are tied to a desk, check our email continually throughout the day.

The Internet. It's revolutionized everything. Life as we know it has changed dramatically in the shadow of its influence – and all in a period of twelve to fourteen years! That's fast. Broken down to its core elements, its all graphics and words. Of course, there's a lot of code behind those graphics and words, but at the end of the day, words are hugely critical for the web to work the way it's supposed to.

So the written word, the *online* written word, is more important than ever. The next question then becomes: how do we use it to communicate effectively? How do we make sure that our intended audience sees it? That's a big part of what this book is about.

As for me, I've always had a love affair with writing. Words are magical to me. For the great mathematical minds of the world, it has been said that they see numbers and calculations in a flash, that they see them dance in their heads and find a way to put them together in new and wonderful ways. That's how it is for me with words. Like a coffee addict making their way once more to Starbucks, I literally am drawn to the computer to put words together. This book is a testament to that! And I love to see how my writing impacts the reader. That's a rush.

For those who are reading this book who happen to be writers, copywriters, or are interested in the art of writing, you can probably say the same thing. And there's probably quite a few of you out there – this book is written for you too.

How did I end up here – writing "Content Rich: Writing Your Way to Wealth on the Web?" I'll give you the short version. It all really started with a dream – the desire to control my destiny, the ability to have something over which I had the ultimate influence. The basics were intact: I believed in myself, I knew what I was capable of. I knew that with the right idea, and the right timing, I could make something a success.

So, I was walking through Barnes and Noble one day and as I went through the aisles, I looked at books in my familiar favorite areas – the biographies, new non-fiction, the music section, the business books. As I was looking through books on marketing, I got to the ones about writing. And there, sitting right there, waiting for me to pick it up, was Bob Bly's "The Copywriters Handbook".[1] Picking up that book became a very important event.

As I paged through the book, I skimmed a few chapters and became immersed in what it was saying. Bob explained how he started a copywriting business twenty years ago and how he was able to turn it into not only a profitable business – but a copywriting *empire*. Through his efforts, he had tapped into a hidden market by writing sales copy for businesses of all kinds. Soon I found out that Bob was a superstar in the industry.

Why was this book such a find for me? "The Copywriters Handbook" explained in detail how to start and run your own copywriting business. It wasn't just about the art of writing, it was telling me step by step how to do this and make some additional income on the side. I had to buy it. I knew this was the key to my new idea.

The week before I stumbled upon Bob's book, I was doing some soul searching. I was trying to do a self evaluation to come up with ideas on what I could do to change and improve my life and my wife's life from a

financial standpoint. I liked real estate, but getting into that took capital
– and luck. The one thing I knew I could do and do as well as the best
out there, was write. Not fiction – but practical *business related* things. I
figured I could write a book some day, maybe a biography since I loved
those so much. I wasn't really thinking about copywriting, until I found
Bob's book. When I bought "The Copywriters Handbook", I was buying
my dream: a way to manage my own financial life.

I read the book in three days. I couldn't put it down! As I read about
how to get started, who you could write for and how much you could be
paid, I knew one thing: *I could do this!* I could make it work, no doubt
about it. I also knew that I would never give up. For me, it all really came
together: my love of writing, my love of starting a business, my dream for a
better life and my MBA experience which gave me good business acumen.
Do what you love and the money will follow, right? There was nothing
more true ever said.

Meanwhile, I had my regular full-time job. The good thing for me
was that I could do this in my spare time. The fact that I was a fast writer
also helped. It's funny, when you have a talent and do something well, you
seem to think that most people are like you. But it's not true. There are
thousands of very successful business people who can't write. To me, that
was an amazing discovery. For me, it meant opportunity. I can *help* these
people; I thought. After all, they are too busy to write. They are running
a business.

Turns out, I was very right about that. And even if I did come across
some potential clients who happened to be great writers, they didn't have
the time or desire to do it. They'd rather play golf and work the sales end
of things, or they would rather build the marketing plan. After looking
around, both in business magazines and online, I realized there was more
copywriting work available than could ever be done in a lifetime. The secret was finding it.

I quickly partnered with a small web design firm and built a website.
I picked a name for the business, "Custom Copywriting." I purchased the
website URL, submitted my DBA (Fictitious Business Name) and got a
business checking account. I got a logo designed for $200 and put it on
business cards, stationary, and envelopes, which I had printed at a local

shop. I used some writing samples from my marketing job for my online portfolio and then approached over forty local non-profits with an offer to write for them for free. That worked well – everyone likes something for free, right? On my lunch time at work, I would meet with these non-profits and talk about newsletters, ads and direct mail letters that they needed written. Within three weeks, I had eight more samples for my website.

Something I did that ended up being a total waste of time was to get the addresses for five hundred ad agencies across the country and send them a letter explaining how I could provide copy for their clients in an over-flow situation or an outsourced arrangement. When I got a response, I sent out a welcome packet that included our samples, a list of fees, some testimonials and a business card. Out of the five hundred letters sent, I got thirty or so inquiries and only one or two actual jobs out of it. I completed those jobs and nothing else ever came from it. But, it was a good lesson. I realized that ad agencies weren't the audience for my service – that was still being developed. I set up accounts on Elance.com and Freelance.com and got business that way for six months or so. Again, it wasn't a very good way to get quality leads, but it served a purpose and led me to the next big thing.

A True Business Developing

Around this time, my wife was going through a lot, dealing with her mother's passing, which had happened the same year I started the business. Through her grieving, she made the decision to see a spiritual medium named Brian Hurst. If you know anything about these guys, you would probably know that Brian was one of the best in the world. Lucky for us, he lived only an hour away in Los Angeles. He was the medium that told the even more well known James Van Praagh that he would one day be a very important Spiritual Medium.

So, I went with her to the reading. She obviously wanted to connect with her mother, which *did* end up happening. For me, this visit was important as well. When it came to my turn, Mr. Hurst said, "Did you just start a business?" I said yes. He said, "Yes, I'm seeing business cards printed up....you've had some success so far, and I want you to know that you NEED to keep doing this." I walked out of there that night knowing that this wasn't just a good idea, it was my destiny!

Now, I had renewed passion. Suddenly, I was on a mission. Within three weeks, I discovered the "next big thing" that I alluded to earlier. The next big thing was Search Engine Optimized (SEO) Web Copy. I had read a bit about it a couple months earlier, but didn't get much out of what I read and for whatever reason, it didn't strike a chord. Once I found the good stuff, I devoured every article and bit of information I could. I went to every site I could find on the web that discussed it. I found out that SEO was part of the "Search Marketing" revolution – the art and science of getting a good position for your website in the natural search rankings. I found out about companies called "search marketing" firms that dedicated their entire business to helping their clients be found on the web. I also realized that this could be Custom Copywriting's specialty. We could be the best in the business. And we could supply these search marketing firms with copy for their clients.

So, that's exactly what we did. First, I found a fantastic web designer who wasn't very expensive to redesign the site. We made sure we optimized for our keyword phrases "web copywriter," "seo copywriting" and all the rest, so we could be found online. Next, I contacted over 200 of the top search marketing companies by email and phone to let them know we could help them save time and money. Most importantly, I wrote five simple articles on the following topics:

- The Future of Advertising
- SEO Copy: The Down and Dirty Details
- Hiring a Great SEO Copywriter
- Ad Copywriting: Building Brand Equity One Word at a Time
- Fixing Bad Website Copy

I read that by writing some articles on relevant topics in your industry and then submitting them to various industry sites, you could get massive free exposure and be seen as an expert in your field. It took me about six hours to write the articles and $100 to have them distributed by a professional – Maria Marsala.[2] Within two weeks, our phone was ringing off the hook. Our business went from $400 a month in sales to $5000 almost over night. My inbox was getting flooded with emails on quote requests and partnership requests. I even got an invitation to have my own segment on a business radio show.

In the next three months, our website secured over 500 quality links back to our site and we started ranking on the 2nd and 3rd page of the Search Engine Results pages (SERP's) for our keyword phrases. Soon enough, we were on the 1st page for big keyword phrases like "copywriting," and on some days, I was getting 25 quote requests. At that moment, I knew we had "lightning in a bottle." Since then, I have written and consulted for hundreds of companies, large and small and impacted sales for just about all of them. We have helped many of those companies achieve higher rankings for their sites and have even brought on additional writers to help with the increased business. My copy has appeared on thousands of web sites, and I have spoken to many business groups on the art and science of SEO Copywriting.

It has been a lot of work – but a lot of fun too. Most of all, I have been able to bring in additional income for my family and help lots of companies succeed. By writing this book, I'm able to help even more people grow their businesses and ultimately, help their families too.

What You'll Learn in "Content Rich – Writing your Way to Wealth on the Web" – Who Should Read this Book?

This book is written to help you connect better with your potential online customers, increase your site's search engine rankings, and/or help you learn the skill of Search Engine Optimized (SEO) web copy. The good thing about all of this is you don't have to be a great writer to start off with; in fact, you don't have to write anything at all if you don't want to. By reading this book, you'll gain an understanding into the power that the right words can have on your site and then you could simply hire someone else to do it for you. My main objective is to transfer some knowledge about web writing to you with the hope that it could make a difference for your business. The other good thing about writing SEO copy is that it's very inexpensive. If you choose to write, it's free. If you choose to outsource, it's still not super expensive. In fact, it really is an *investment*. You'll see a return on investment in as short as a month or two. That's not bad. Plus, once you achieve higher rankings and higher sales, it will then simply be a question of maintaining that level of success and increasing it if you'd like to generate an even higher level of sales.

Were you aware that 75-80% of all web traffic comes from the search engines?

B to B Magazine said, "Studies have shown that second or third page rankings can increase Web site traffic by up to nine times. Top 10 rankings, or first page listings, can mean an additional sixfold increase in traffic. The correlating impact on sales is also astronomical: 42% more sales within the first month of Top 10 listings and nearly 100% more the second month." [3]

One thing to keep in mind, however, is that writing some SEO copy is only one portion of an overall site optimization effort. You'll also need to probably improve the design of your site and have a professional work on the coding to make sure it's SEO friendly as well. Things like having a site map, using alt tags, and balancing the copy with the site's images. All of this is just as important as writing the copy.

So, who is the book for exactly? If you are a new business or have a small business, it's definitely for you. Making sure your website connects with your prospects is critical – every lead is important. You never know where your big lead is going to come from. If you're a small business, you either:

- Don't have a website
- Have a website but need some improvements in search rankings
- Have a website but need some help in converting prospective customers into sales.
- Have a website but need help in search rankings and sales conversion.

If your small business operates exclusively on the web, then this book is even more important for you. And it doesn't matter whether you sell a product or a service – SEO web copy can help both.

If you are a large corporation, you probably have a marketing department and IT (Information Technology) department. One or the other or both probably maintain the content you have on the website. But are they doing an effective job? Do they really know search engine optimization? Do they understand the power of search marketing? Most marketing folks are dialed into print advertising and market research, but it's surprising how many don't know enough about the web and marketing on the web to take real advantage. After all, there wouldn't be thousands of people from the marketing and IT departments of major corporations going to the highly successful Search Engine Strategies conference[4] every year to learn about it if there wasn't a knowledge gap out there. In addition, small web upstarts wouldn't be able to achieve higher rankings on the search engines than the GE's, Fords and Panasonics of the world if there wasn't a need. And then there's the issue of having too many other things to do besides maintaining the content on the corporate sites. Outsourcing it is a smart decision – and these corporations can remain focused on their core competencies.

The bottom line is that corporations everywhere can benefit from learning about what's in this book. SEO copywriting can help you in big ways too.

If you are an individual who has a site for business or pleasure, SEO copywriting can help you as well. That's part of the reason why blogs have become so big. If you're doing it right, you are using the techniques of search engine optimization on your blog, including using the most appropriate keywords, tags and links to get search engine traffic. The most successful blog writers are masters of SEO copywriting. If you're not selling anything, you may want to build an online community through your site. Social networking online has become a multi-billion dollar industry in its own right over the past few years. All of this building of online communities is huge when it comes to SEO copywriting. You can connect with people all over the world for hundreds of different reasons, all by ensuring that the words you use on your site mean something to them.

Finally, if you are a writer yourself and want to learn the basics of SEO copywriting, this book is most definitely for you. Every day, I receive resumes from writers all over the world who are seeking to get into the profession. They may be writers already, they may have just written a great piece of fiction, or they may be new to writing altogether. Whatever their backgrounds, there are a lot of writers out there and plenty of SEO copy for them to work on. With all the millions of sites now online and the millions more coming in the future, you can see this is a business that is not going away any time soon. This book will give you all the basics of writing solid copy - copy that *converts* and helps to *improve rankings*. It also will provide the details you need on how to write better SEO copy.

So, if you are a marketing manager, content editor, site owner, small business person, online retailer, SEO project manager, public relations professional, ad agency, Corporate VP of Marketing, web designer or copywriter, this book is for YOU!

What specifically will you be able to take away after reading this book?

First, you'll get to know all the details on writing general site copy – your Home page, the About Us page, Products or Services pages, FAQ's and all the other types of pages that you may be utilizing on your website. There are certain things you'll need to do and certain things you'll want to avoid and little tricks you can employ that will give you an instant advantage. We'll go over *all* of that.

You'll also learn how to write articles for your business - articles that can be distributed across the web to give you instant credibility in your industry. You'll find out what types of topics would be interesting to your target audience, which types of articles get picked up by article sites, and how you get business from the article. You'll also understand the viral nature of your articles and how they can keep building your customer base long after you have written them.

Web articles serve the same function as writing traditional articles for a magazine and discussing a topic relevant to your industry. Except with web articles, you'll find very little submission rejection, quicker response to your article and potentially much more exposure, all over the world. That's a little different from the magazine article writing experience! There's just

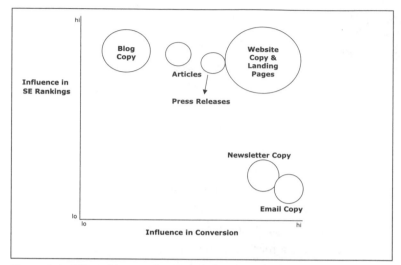

Figure 1-1: Different types of content influence search engine rankings
and sales conversion in different ways.

something magical that happens when people read your article, get something valuable from it without having to pay anything for the information
and then see your name attached to it. Automatically, *you* are the expert.

This book will also show you how to write optimized press releases.
These little juggernauts of Internet marketing gold can make big changes,
very fast. It's already a good thing you have something positive that you
want to announce to the world. What's great about the SEO part of press
releases is that your release can be picked up by all types of news organizations and other sites for free publicity. You never know what sites those
may be. There's always a few that will surprise you, and many times, those
are the ones that email you after they see it and end up buying something
from you. Some press release sites out there like PR Web[5] even offer a low
cost submission feature, so you don't have to pay much for the publicity.
But, it's always better to pay to have it sent out to all of the major press
organizations. More about that in chapter 8.

Other types of SEO copy that you'll learn about are email copy, blog
copy, pay per click ad copy and "direct response" sales letter web copy. All
of them have a role to play in your SEO web marketing arsenal. As well,
many sites can use every single one of them. It's not enough to just write
high quality copy for your website; you need to write value added articles,

emails that convert and press releases that make you shine as well. But you'll learn all of that in due time. I'm anxious to help facilitate the learning process!

But Wait, there's More!

Content Rich has been a labor of love, a true extension of my passion for writing, teaching and helping other businesses succeed. So, I'm doing something that few, if any, writers ever do. In the spirit of shareware, Skype[6], and altruistic business people everywhere, I want to offer you something more than just the book. You already have given me something more than I ever thought I would get a chance to give – you purchased this book! And I sincerely thank you for that. I hope you get a lot out of it. But in addition to receiving this book, you also get the following:

- Free online access to the next two editions

- A free audio program that discusses key topics from this book by profiling certain SEO copy business case studies

- A free online video of a recent performance of the live version of Content Rich

- A complimentary web site copy inspection

- 30% discounts on any marketing consulting and/or Content Rich Live Seminar programs for the next two years (2008-2009)

So, there you have it. The keys to the SEO copy kingdom! And there's no catch. I don't know about you, but I *hate* gimmicks. Access to your audio program, live *Content Rich* video and other free online bonus items are right here, included in your book order. Simply send an email to readers@contentrichbook.com and we'll be sure you receive your free items!

I'm excited to have this opportunity with you! I think you're going to really enjoy the topics covered in the book. I can honestly say I've really enjoyed putting "pen to paper"…or the more often utilized "fingers to keyboard." It has been a labor of love.

After you complete it, feel free to send me an email and tell me what you thought. I always like to know what made the biggest impact on people and what could use some improvement. It's the only way we get better.

So, let's get started… What is SEO Copywriting all about?

SEO Copywriting:
The Basics

Part I

What is Search Engine Optimized (SEO) Web Copy?

So, what is this thing called Search Engine Optimized Web Copy? Many of us, some of you even reading this book, already know what it is. You've worked with it, written some, done a bit of research and know what it's capable of doing. But do you know where it's going? Where it may take us? The impact of writing copy for Internet video? How about all the types of SEO copy that can be written? Are you aware of social media copy optimization, long-tail optimization, tagging and the nuances of blog copy creation? There's a lot to know about this ever-growing thing called SEO web copy. So, again, the question: What is it?

Search Engine Optimization is the practice of using a variety of techniques to improve a site's ranking on the search engines. These things could include editing or adding to HTML code, working with site navigation features, employing linking strategies, and last but not least – what this book is all about: *web page copywriting*.

The words and phrases you choose to use impact the overall picture of a web site's success like never before. As in the dawn of the industrial age, where one discovery seemed to lead to another and another in quick succession, so too is the quickly evolving mystery and magic of optimized website copywriting.

And it's a serious business. Literal fortunes are being made online. Businesses that never competed – or partnered with each other before - are now doing so. Cross pollination, business hybrids, new and exciting technologies, co-branding: they are all being impacted in a big way by the words that make up the web. The exciting part is that its impact on culture and commerce is just beginning. The really great thing about all of this is that people – of a wide diversity are being brought together and being forced to interact. For example: when would I have talked to a business-man from Hong Kong if he hadn't contacted me after finding my site on a search? Who knew that international online commerce would break down the walls that separated us?

OK, it's not going to bring about world peace and total global nir-vana, but it's a positive and somewhat unexpected result, right? The one thing you can be sure of is that I take it seriously. I have seen first hand how businesses have been impacted by the words I have written for their sites. It's a shame when a third generation corner bakery in Tallahassee, Florida, still hasn't bought into the power of the web and chooses to throw their advertising dollars away by doing yet another direct mail piece that only brings in a paltry 1% response rate. There's a better way! Or, at least, a way that should be *investigated* at the very least. That bakery could put up a website, do a series of combination direct mail/email offers, optimize their site and draw business from local searches.

It still surprises me when I go to a business group's meeting to speak on the topics of *Content Rich* and see some blank faces staring back at me, as if they are hearing this information for the very first time. I suspect that many of them are. Of course, I may be the challenged one, thinking that most people out there know the basics of writing for the web. But, this is about making money! And helping businesses be successful by taking shortcuts to that success. The dynamic of people searching for goods and services on the web is only going to increase. How about getting in on some of that action? How about doing it for free?! It can be done! It's done everyday.

It also amazes me how many sites out there are in such desperate need of new copy/content. If you are a copywriter or want to be one, you could start your business by being a little proactive and approaching companies that you think could benefit from your wordsmithing. Just start searching for something and pick a few. Send them an email. Tell them to give you a chance at improving their content. Show them past successes. Indicate that they will pay nothing if your changes don't make a positive impact. I guarantee you could build a copywriting business this way.

The mere *idea* shows the sheer potential that SEO copywriting and the Internet have for the future. But getting back to the topic at hand - the fact that so many sites out there need copy help... what exactly are those companies thinking? Hasn't anyone ever told them they need more than twenty words on their home page? Where's the courageous friend who will level with their business buddy by nicely letting them know that their copy needs to be written grammatically correct and with a call to action?

A Short History of the Words that Make Up the Web

Way back when in 1995, at the dawn of this thing called the World Wide Web, there was no clear picture of where this all was heading. No one really knew how sites should look, how they would be found, and which ones to trust. It was total turmoil, an exercise in trial and error, a struggle between assumed power brokers, trying to jockey for control of a piece of the pie. Some people got ripped off and others made lots of money. Mistakes were made, opportunities realized. All of this is true as it relates to the copy that helped make up the early web. Was one long page of copy on the home page an accepted format? Or were a hundred small pages with a paragraph or snippet of copy more popular? Over time, this all got ironed out, but the web was a confusing place to be twelve to thirteen years ago; it was also very exciting.

At the time, a webmaster would simply submit a page to the search engines. The search engines would "crawl" the page with what was called a "spider" which would pull links to other pages from that page. It would then return information found on the page to be indexed. An "indexer" filtered information about the page, including *the words* that were on the page. How many words, which words were repeated, where the words were located and any weight for specific words. Of course, the value of a highly ranked site was something that took hold rapidly. Just like today, everyone wanted lots of traffic.

The problem is that people started looking for shortcuts. They tried to rig the system and manipulate certain variables. Search algorithms were based on keyword Meta tags and other similar devices that provided a guide to a web page's content. This was a poorly conceived idea because it encouraged the tricky and unethical behavior that I'm referencing: webmasters would misuse Meta tags by including irrelevant keywords to artificially increase page impressions for their website, among other "black hat" SEO copy behaviors. Search engines reacted to this by attempting to develop more complex and better ranking algorithms.

Enter the Dragon: Google

Google started to come into prominence in 1998 due to their unique approach to SEO copy and website rankings. Their algorithm included looking at the links that were pointing towards a site and how prominent those links were. This wasn't the only variable that made up their algorithm, but it was the most important. In time, they developed the "Pagerank" concept and that changed everyone's perception of a website's copy and its subsequent ranking. Of course, there was attempted abuse with this new dynamic as well, but it was much harder to game by unscrupulous web designers and programmers. Today, Google still leads the charge as it pertains to the effect and impact that SEO copy and other variables play. The good thing is that we've come a long way in a short amount of time.

Everyday that goes by, the web becomes better, stronger, larger, and more secure. But human nature being what it is, there will always be people out there trying to find a way to break the rules. The great thing about using SEO copy is that it can *seem* like you're breaking the rules when you realize how systematic and easy it can be if you just follow the advice this book offers. Trust me: you won't be breaking the rules, but you'll be happy to know that you can make an impact – today.

SEO Content Search Engines
Speaks to   & People

Serving Two Masters

Now that we know what SEO copy is and a little bit about its history, we need to bring up another critical point: it serves two masters. The two masters we are referring to of course are the Search Engines and the potential Customer who has found your site. They both have unique needs. The search engines are asking you to use certain keyword phrases a few times, in a few certain places and on a few different pages. The customer is asking for benefits – what's this gym going to do for me if I join it? How is a membership to the Sunset Wine Club[7] different or better than signing up for Cameron Hughes'[8] Wine Club? They couldn't care less whether you've used a certain set of words 4.5 times, especially at the top of the page and in the sub-headers and Meta tags. (more on that later!) Many "regular" people out there don't have any idea what SEO is all about anyway.

The big fallacy and controversy out there in recent years is that you *can't* serve these two masters simultaneously. That's crazy. It's purely ridiculous. *Of course* you can. It's actually fairly straightforward. There's a system to it, a certain way of approaching it, of course; but it can be done, with no problem whatsoever. Those who claim it's difficult or can't be done effectively for both just don't get it. The problem really comes down to this fact: there are a lot of bad copywriters out there. Yes, believe it or not, there are web writers who claim to be very good at SEO who plainly are not. These are the ones that make it look like it can't be done. They don't know what they're doing!

Different Sites Need Unique Types of Copy

If you are a law firm, do you need copy written for a Shopping Cart web page? Probably not. Likewise, if you are operating a website that manufactures guitars and you have a network of retailers, do you need to write copy that discusses pricing of certain models? Not really. Let the retailers do that. If you are running a Japanese restaurant, do you need to use SEO articles, blog copy, and press release copy? Probably not. I mean, you could do a blog I guess, but how would that affect your brand? Is it necessary? Not really. If you are an advertising agency or search marketing firm, I would say, hands down, yes! The fact is that every site has unique needs as it pertains to SEO copy. There's no "one size fits all." But be careful not to totally disregard a new type of web copy because at first glance it looks like it may not be applicable to you.

Take copy for website videos, ala You Tube[9] on your home page, a quick video message from your CEO or VP of Customer Service perhaps. There are many businesses that may think this type of thing wouldn't belong on their site. I would say that most sites would be wise to consider it. Most Internet experts say it's going to be a big part of the future web. Same with those animated images of real people that are popping up on a few cool sites out there, telling you why their product is the greatest thing in the world - they're on stage right there on your laptop screen for crying out loud. What a great concept. And you know what? Script copy needs to be written for these too! It never ends!

Another strategy that could be employed with your SEO web writing is to use it to compliment and support online behavior. Most of us know that the web makes us act or behave in certain ways that are unique only to this medium. Its sole individuality probably spawns this. When television came out, people probably received the information that was being communicated in different ways from radio, for example. With radio, of course, there was more left up to the imagination when audio was the *only* component. Along comes the talking box known as TV, and wham! Everything changed. We could see the meaning behind those spoken words, because we could see the person speaking them. At least, we could assume the meaning. Now with the Internet and web writing, we have audio, video, good old fashioned reading, and something entirely new – an interactive dynamic. It's two way communication. Its not that way with radio and TV, right? (At least this is true generally.)

Then there is the way the information is actually processed. I already mentioned that we "scan" read on the web, unlike a newspaper, magazine or book. People don't want to work that hard, right? Well, to our credit, we are busy and don't have the time to read every word. There's no need to if you can get the meaning from scanning it in a quarter of the time and get 90% of the meaning. But here's the key: we need to *make* the copy simple to scan! Many sites are making the mistake of not making their copy scan-friendly.

In addition, online shopping is not really a true "browsing" experience. Yes, we look around and surf from site to site, but unlike retail stores, where we can window shop, go in and pick up the item, touch and feel it, online shoppers really are "directed." People go on to a site and utilize the search box to find a very specific product. This is what could be called a *directed* approach. Knowing this, we want to make the copy more succinct, segmented and specific so we can help the customer to buy quicker and easier. This is a good thing to know. Its a little tough to employ at first, but helpful because we always need to be reminded to tailor the copy we write to the way humans act and behave.

If we were to look at all the types of sites on the Internet, there seems to be a simple way to categorize them based on user experience, goals of the site and the way products/services are sold. So, let's use the following grouping for site types:

- Blogs/Social Networking Sites

- E-commerce sites

- Lead Generation/Sales Sites

- "Brochure" Sites (the main selling is not done on the website)

There are probably other types of sites that you could identify and sub-categories of each, but for our purposes, this works well. In terms of SEO copywriting and the types of content you need, you'll see that there are some types that are more important or take on greater meaning than others.

As you read through the rest of *Content Rich*, keep this diagram in mind. The goal is to get you thinking in terms of the "total online SEO copywriting universe" and to see that different types of optimized content can serve you in different ways.

Content Importance Ranked (Type of Site)

	E-Commerce	Blogs/Social Networking	Brochure	Lead Generation
1	site	blog	site	site
2	video/podcast	video/podcast	newsletter	email
3	email	newsletter	email	newsletter
4	newsletter	email	blog	articles
5	blog		press release	press release
6	article		article	blog
7	press release		video/podcast	video/podcast

Taking this discussion a step further, we should also mention that SEO copy is used to reassure, and calm people's concerns. When we look at the most important factors that keep people from engaging in more online shopping[10], what do we see? What they say is:

- Sites/carts are too complicated – 14%
- Return/exchange policies – 41%
- Fraud/Identity Theft – 49%
- Sharing Personal Info - 53%

So, what is SEO copy? It's a means of ***communicating confidence and integrity on behalf of an online business***. All of these factors can be addressed through the copywriting process. The sections you write and the words you choose can be decided upon by looking at each of these reasons and then coming up with the best language to provide a good feeling in the prospective customer's mind. One thing to consider however: the more often a person shops online, the less significant these concerns become.

So what's the bottom line? Make sure you write a Privacy page on your site, organize the copy in logical fashion, and reassure the customer that their information won't be sold to anyone else. In essence, make them feel comfortable to do business with you. You're not there in person to shake their hand, make direct eye contact and tell them it will "all be ok," so make sure your copy does that for you.

SEO Copy and Some Interesting Online Statistics

Consider this statistic: Search Marketing will be a $7 Billion business this year[11]. If that doesn't tell you that you should be focused on search engine optimized content, I'm not sure what would. After all, copy is a huge part of the equation. What's it going to be next year or the year after? Whether you are a copywriter yourself or running an online business, it's time for your website's words to shine! What is SEO copy? It's knowing that adding wikis, RSS, and tags to your content are all really great ideas. If these are all new terms for you, no worries. We'll get to each one in detail so you can see how they may impact your site's performance.

People can learn about a website from a lot of different sources. They can see it advertised on a bus, get a brochure given to them by a friend, or see it on a business card. For the ten categories in the next chart, much of their traffic came from the search engines themselves. What is the lesson for those of you in these areas? To write copy that appeals to the lovely little engines!

What about local searches (people looking online for goods and services in their home town)? What kind of important stats can we uncover in terms of SEO copywriting for your sites? Well, how about the top keywords utilized in local searches? That sounds like a good one. (See the chart on the next page.) Again, if you operate an online business in any one of these categories, you have a lot of upside when it comes to ensuring the content on your site is fully optimized. Read on my friend!

The "Content Rich Quotient" (CRQ)

The Content Rich Quotient is a measurement tool I developed to help companies understand where they are relative to their competitors and to determine where they are along the path of their online copywriting evolution. It also shows how current they are with what's happening in search marketing and SEO copywriting. Essentially, it's made up of four key areas, each one having a unique importance to the total CRQ score. These four areas are:

Top Industries Reached by Search Engines [12]

1. Health and medical – 43%
2. Education – 40%
3. Food and beverage – 37%
4. Government – 31%
5. Community – 30%
6. Travel – 28%
7. Music – 27%
8. Shopping and classified – 25%
9. Aviation – 21%
10. Automotive – 21%

- **Content Breadth Factor:** This analytic places importance on how many types of web content you are utilizing and how qualitative they are in terms of user benefit and SEO factors. What are the types of content we are referring to? Website, Article, Press Release, Blog, Pay Per Click and Newsletters. Of course, not all businesses and other organizations will need all of these online vehicles, but I personally believe many could benefit from each of them in one way or another.

- **Social Media Optimization (SMO)/Search Engine Optimization (SEO) Balance:** SMO, as we will discuss in a later chapter, is all about making changes to optimize a site so that it is more easily linked to, more highly visible in social media searches on custom search engines like Technorati, and more frequently included in relevant posts on blogs, podcasts and vlogs. SMO is a relatively new development over the past 18 months. SEO,

The Top Keywords for Local Searches [13]:

1. Real Estate
2. Restaurants
3. Dentists
4. Computer Repair
5. Plumbers
6. Lasik
7. DUI Attorney
8. Hotels

which has been around longer, is the practice of using a variety of techniques to improve a site's ranking on the search engines. By doing both of these things well, you are helping to build rich content.

Keywords Searched - Breakdown[14]

1 Word Searched – 23%
(Example: Motorcycles)

2 Words Searched – 26%
(Example: Harley Motorcycles)

3 Words Searched – 21%
(Example: Harley Davidson Motorcycles)

• **Content Effectiveness Measurement:** Analyze peoples path through your site. Where are they just before they go to the order page or contact page? Which content is making the most impact? How many people are responding or reacting to your content? And how many content types are they responding to? You'll need to study your web analytics program and/or ask them to find out, but this is extremely valuable information.

• **The Content "Clincher":** Which specific language/copy is truly responsible for the sale (or conversion)? If it was online content that converted a prospect (and not a personal conversation, phone interaction, direct mailer, etc) then wouldn't you want to know which exact words, feature/benefit statements or specials made them say YES? Whatever it was, this would be known as the Content Clincher, the last attribute of the CRQ. If online content never converts prospects, well

Number of Pages Looked at Before a Search is Concluded[15]

First Page: 39%
First Two Pages: 19%
First Three Pages: 9%
More than Three Pages: 10%

then your score for this would be "0". The more different types of clinchers you have, the higher your score.

The Content Rich Quotient is a mix of subjective and objective scoring, but is very basic to understand and score. The total possible high score is 12.

This would represent a site that is very content rich. Each of the four attributes has a possible score of 3.

Here is a simple example of how the scoring works:

The company is LightSpeed Printing. They have been online for five years and are doing some things very well, others not so good. For their **Content Breadth Factor** they scored a 2: they have high quality SEO copy across the board, but are missing article content. For **SMO/SEO Balance**, they got a 1: SEO is top notch, they do everything right with this one. But SMO is something they are a bit challenged with; they do have some great linking and have a well received blog, but don't do any vlogs or podcasts yet. For their **Content Effectiveness Measurement**, they got a 3: many forms of their online copy are making an impact. Sales materialize from their website, newsletters, blog and press releases. There isn't one specific content type that is driving all the conversion benefit. Finally, for their **Content Clincher**, they got a 2: they know which benefit statements are converting people and most of their sales come from online copy, but there's still room for improvement.

Their final CRQ is 8 - a good score. What would yours be? Score yourself honestly.

Summing it All Up

SEO Copywriting means a lot of different things to a lot of people. For those in the know, they understand how powerful it can really be. Perhaps they run a data recovery business, have written ten articles on unique topics, distributed them out to the web, and have seen a 15% jump in business directly attributed to the articles. Or maybe they are a new site from an American company that was optimized by a professional firm and all of a sudden they are getting new clients from Europe. Whatever the success story, there are many being told. Words have meaning. When they appear on your website, they have even more depth. The next question then becomes *Why*.

CHAPTER REVIEW

- Search Engine Optimization is the practice of using a variety of techniques to improve a site's ranking on the search engines.

- SEO website copy serves two simultaneous functions: helps the search engines find your pages and "speaks" to your customers in a compelling way.

- Different types of websites require unique forms of copy – a retail site needs to discuss product benefits, a service site needs to explain customer support.

- Online copywriting and search engine metrics go hand in hand – be sure to stay on top of the numbers to see how your copy is impacting users.

- The Content Rich Quotient can be a very effective tool to measure your SEO copywriting progress, be sure to take a look at it for your online content.

Next: Why does SEO copy work? Well, let's look into it.

CHAPTER 2

WHY DOES SEO CONTENT WORK?

Words are the lifeblood of the Internet, it's what you see when you are surfing the web, it's what you read when you are browsing, buying, or shopping. Words are so important to the web that some sites *only have* words – no pictures, no graphics, no eye candy. This of course, is a mistake. All words and no imagery make for one big, boring website. Those that take this approach seem very bent on providing lots of information, tons of detail about every nuance of their product or service. They may not have any real web design ability or perhaps they didn't want to pay someone to do it. Perhaps they got a hold of Microsoft Front Page, and just started going to work. They may have been looking for an easy way to get their site up or started with the intention of adding pictures later. I think we can all agree that the visual representation of your site needs to be a *combination* of words and graphics – robust content that you continue to build on over time.

So *why* does SEO content work? How does this massive information source, known as the World Wide Web wield the power that it does? The easiest and most obvious answer is that people want to *connect.* We want to communicate, share new information and build bridges. We want to meet new people. Yes, we want to sell something many times, but behind that is the need to develop and build a relationship – to connect with another human being on some level. Once you begin to connect with someone via a website, it becomes empowering, both for the communicator and the recipient of the communication. At that point, anything can happen. Information can be transferred and delivered. Ideas can be generated. And if you want, you can choose *not to* communicate at all. It very well could be a one-way information source.

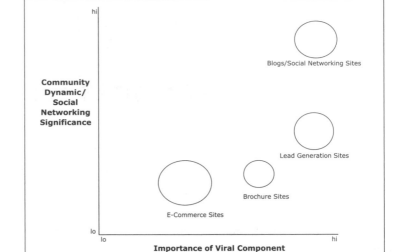

It is Currency to the Search Engines

Why does SEO content work? The biggest reason is because it's *what the search engines pay attention to,* or at least a big part of what they pay attention to. They consider it important, plain and simple. It goes into how the search engines measure success and relevance. It drives the need to have search marketing firms manage pay per click and natural search campaigns. They also look at lots of other things too – the number of links pointing back to your site, the length of time you've had your site up, whether you have a site map or not; all of these factors, and more, play a role in the overall search engine optimization effort. But words, *SEO words,* are key.

So, we play the game. We build big, beautiful, content rich sites and hope that people will find us. We build out the site to include pages and pages of useful articles and other information about our product or service. We start blogs and are careful to update them as frequently as possible.

The majority of us of course *don't* do these things – either we don't have the time, the desire, the capital or the ability to do it. If this describes you, then you are reading the right book! We'll make all those concerns go away. There's a good solution for all of them. And it's a lot easier than you may think.

A nice thing to know is that Google and Yahoo and all the others will always consider SEO content to be very important. It's something that we can truly count on – and work on as long as we have a site to update. Of course, knowing that is great, but how do we make sure it's the content they want, that they will pay attention to consistently? Read on! We'll get to all of that, one type of content at a time. Whether you want to know about the inner workings of your site copy, the effect that articles will have on your business, or want to polish your email communications to customers, you'll have a new understanding and appreciation for all of it in no time.

Helps Bring Different Personalities Together

Acting alone, you can get all types of information about a particular product or service you are inquiring about and choose to purchase something or not, to contact them for more information, or not. The power is with **you**, the searcher. Carrying this further, we could even discuss personality differences between extroverted and introverted people. If you think about it, the web essentially levels the playing field between them. As the power of the written word has risen, so too has the effectiveness of the more introverted personality - people can communicate without ever seeing each other. This has significant implications for how people communicate and get things done together.

So, why does SEO content work? Partially because an entire group of people, (20% of us apparently) who previously felt alienated in social business situations, can now "talk" to others in a way that never existed before. To communicate your point via email impacts this dynamic as well. Before the Internet, these people had a difficult time exerting any significant influence or power over business decision making.

Of course, there are exceptions to every rule, but for the most part, this dynamic applies. As a shy person myself, I can attest to it. Opening my copywriting shop as a brick and mortar retail business would have proven much more difficult. Challenging, of course, for many unique reasons, but most challenging because I would have had to interface with people all day long, which would have physically and emotionally exhausted me. With the magic of the web, my website and emails utilizing SEO content, I can go all day long and have energy left at the end of the day. Plus, I can choose when I want to interact with people face to face.

Allows for Quick Changes

Another reason why SEO content works is because it can be updated immediately. It can be altered, added to, subtracted from and built out whenever you like, all at the click of a mouse. This provides a lot of options. If a customer brings up an important benefit that your service is not addressing, you can make a change in the language – and automatically be offering the service that went unoffered the day before. Who knows, that key service may be the one that grows your business into the stratosphere. After all, we don't really know what business we're in until our customers tell us, right? They ultimately will be the communicator of this information.

In the same way, if you find out that a competitor is successfully using a few keyword phrases that your site is missing; you can add those to your pages and your Meta tags and position your site to compete with them on those same keyword phrases. Although it may take a few weeks to make a big impact, you still have the power to make this edit with the dynamic of SEO copy.

In the information age, people are hungry for new ideas and new trends. They gobble up data with a speed unheard of during the Industrial Age. Things change fast and these changes are driven by the customer. Like the spread and ultimate triumph of democracy, the power of the Internet and SEO copy along with it - *is with the people*. This power is being exercised at unprecedented levels. Which brings up another reason why SEO content works – it puts the customer, the buyer, *the people* in control. Instead of a "push" strategy where you are forcing your product or service on people and hoping they respond (with a direct mail piece, telemarketing program or television ad), websites and the SEO content that is contained in them provides for more of a "pull" dynamic, where the customer decides almost everything. As the business person, you win, of course, because the customers who get to your site, read your copy and decide they want to find out more are *prequalified*.

Of course, there's a lot you'll have to do to get your site in a place where the customer will find you, but if you do this and do it well, you could share something that my business, Custom Copywriting, enjoys - very little advertising expense! That just makes it all easier and a better experience for your customer too. The direct mail and other traditional ways of advertising and communicating will probably never stop (actually they will continue to proliferate), but the online medium and the SEO content that tells the story will be the most powerful.

A Reflection of Human Behavior

If you think about it, the web is really a microcosm of human behavior itself. It mimics the best of us and the worst of us, the most daring ideas and some of the weak ones too. Plus, if there is something like the Internet that can help us fulfill our goals and life ambitions in a much easier way, why not jump on it, right? The sheer efficiency of the web and the words that it delivers is offering a quicker path to success and happiness for those that embrace it. At the very least, it is providing a complimentary communication channel to the traditional ones used by industries of the past. Even businesses that never thought they could have a web presence or would even need a web presence have discovered that they were wrong. If they thought the web was a passing fad or that their products or services couldn't be sold on the web, that was just bad thinking, plain and simple. Yes, it's probably true that Bob's corner grocery store and Philips and Temroe, Attorneys at Law, won't actually sell something via their website, but they can provide lots of detailed information about what they offer, so when prospective customers or clients are knocking on their door, they have a means to answer it.

As the ultimate competitive space, this arena of content and virtual communication can make a company known practically overnight – and undo them just as fast. SEO Content keeps us honest. We can almost tell what a business is all about after simply reading their home page, right?

How many times was a nice couple led astray when they walked into a car dealership and purchased a new vehicle in the pre-Internet days? A conniving, persuasive salesperson would use every tricky verbal strategy and set of spoken words to get them to sign on the dotted line. The sheer personality of the sales person could almost direct the entire transaction. And what happened? The nice couple ended up with the wrong car at the wrong price and with the wrong terms. Today, that couple doesn't need to even step foot in the sleazy car dealership, they can read all about it online, on the dealership's website, compare them to others and make a decision based on the facts – not someone's spoken words and charismatic personality. The customer wins – and ultimately, the dealership wins too. They don't have to deal with an unhappy customer three months down the road.

Plus, there's a third party – Google – helping to show you who the best dealership's websites are. Chances are if they are operating shady enterprises in the retail store environment, they are probably doing the same online. If the search engines pick up on it, which many times, they do, that site will be banned from the web. You win then too.

The Competitive Force

This leads us to another reason why writing words on your site works so well. It provides for greater competition and increases your ability to compete. Greater competition stirs the very passion of people. It ignites their potential. It stimulates their drive to excel. Similar to the airlines fighting over your business by having airfare wars, or local banks offering totally free checking to get you to open an account, everyone wins when websites compete through their content. The smart business will look at their competitor's sites – and what they are saying on their sites on a regular basis. The savvy online enterprise monitors the content of their toughest rivals all the time. They check the Meta tags, any new pages, new offerings, the keyword phrases and anything else they can to get an advantage.

Being at the very top spot on page one for your most important keyword phrase can bring in thousands of dollars very quickly and be a reason why a customer picks you instead of the next guy. In the same way, if a company doesn't focus on search engine optimization, but has a great story to tell and shows their concern for their customers in the words they use and the testimonials they provide, this can be equally important. It's not only about search engine rankings. Lots of companies at the very top, who didn't focus on conversion once a customer got to the site, have paid the price.

How about the cost savings? How expensive do you think it was for a furniture store to print up full color, ten page brochures and have them sent out to 5,000 prospective customers in 1985? Probably in the neighborhood of $15,000. How expensive is it for that same furniture store to put together a basic website, write the content, ensure its search engine optimized and promote it to 500,000 or more? Probably $5,000. Reaching three to hundreds of times the amount of customers for a third of the cost. That not only makes good business sense, it makes the world a more efficient place to live in. It's not just the content that gets optimized; the energy expended is optimized as well.

If you choose to write the content for your site on your own, that's even more of a bonus. This, of course, would be free, minus the time you spent writing it. The web is like a living, breathing thing that evolves and provides for a dynamic user experience. Once you build a site and write the copy, then it simply becomes a matter of keeping it fresh and updating it when necessary. If you're not doing it, make sure you are capitalizing on the cost savings that SEO content can provide you.

SEO Content Fosters Comparison Shopping

Why else does SEO content work? Because it provides for easy comparison between companies, products and services. How great is it that the top ten optimized sites with the top ten levels of quality content are all on the first two pages of your online search? (Doesn't always happen of course.) How nice is it that you can hop over to Epinions.com or PriceGrabber.com and check previous customer experiences and the best prices? You can check prices on lawnmowers at Wal-Mart, Target and Home Depot side by side, or check the availability of a book at Barnes and Noble, your local bookstore and Amazon.com all within five minutes.

SEO content and the direct comparison it can show, provides for a customer-centric approach, makes business easier, and in the end, really improves the human condition. How? Because we're finding more and better ways to communicate with more people – more in terms of number and more in terms of diversity. Everyone wins in that scenario.

SEO Content also has a viral component to it. This is a *huge* reason why it works so well. If you run a cooking website that happens to also sell kitchen appliances and decide one day to post a new set of articles on healthy dessert recipes, your articles can show up on thousands of other cooking sites in a matter of a couple of weeks, or a couple of days if it's popular information. Of course, you need to write the content, offer it up for the taking (with a link back to your site), and distribute it out to the web, but this is easy when compared to the means of publicity in the pre-Internet days. Back then, we had to rely on a sales force, a branding campaign and/or expensive brochures and trade shows to get the word out. Now the word – the written word – is driving sales in unique ways, through exciting viral methods, unimagined in the days of traditional advertising.

It also helps to have greater access to the very best in us – the desire to give back and to connect with the less fortunate. Whether it's your favorite charity or finding out about local church groups, SEO content is there to help you find what you are looking for. The Salvation Army website has content that explains how you can contribute in your local community. They also have information on frequently asked questions, tax benefits, and profiles of people who have been helped by donations. When you are on a site like this and you can read everything there is to know about a group like the Salvation Army, you feel like you know what drives them, and your donation will go to the right group. Along the way, you can actually help another person and feel better about yourself too. SEO content can deliver positive impact for many different social causes.

Expanding Your Sales Base

Finally, SEO content works because of one other very important reason – *it provides the means to expand your reach exponentially to new customers, all over the globe (or in your local area)*. In fact, we could have started with this benefit at the beginning of the chapter; it's just as significant as one of the other reasons why SEO content works - the fact that the search engines consider it important. But, I chose to end the chapter with this one because it will help you remember its importance.

The first thing to consider when thinking about how this impacts your business is this: who is my target audience? If you run a barber shop in Seattle, you aren't trying to get clients from the middle of Indiana or the French Riviera. So, you tailor your site content to reflect this. You use geographic language in the SEO copy so when someone searches for "haircuts in Seattle," you show up at the top of the search results. This would be called *tailoring the content for local search*. If you've followed any of the search marketing news over the last couple of years, you know that local search is probably the fastest growing segment out there. If you are a local barber shop in Seattle, or a florist in a small town in Saskatchewan, Canada, be sure you read chapter 12: *SEO Copywriting for Small/Medium Sized Businesses* and chapter 17: *The Future of SEO Copywriting: The Future is Now.*

At the same time, if you sell business software that helps companies manage inventory and logistics, your audience can truly be global. This is where it gets very exciting. For our company, I never dreamed that my writers and I would be designing business prose for websites in Australia and the UK. In the beginning, I thought it would be nice to just write part time for a few local ad agencies. But, the power of my SEO content was there, waiting to take me on a ride that I didn't even know about. I put it out there, and the search engines and people everywhere did the rest. That's what I call a true, participatory e-commerce experience! It also helped provide an entirely new revenue stream, and helped me provide a down payment on a house and pay for expensive medical treatments for my family. So, why does SEO content work? Because it ultimately impacts the very things that are most important in our lives: the people we love.

CHAPTER REVIEW

- SEO content works because it's what the search engines pay attention to; they consider it critically important.

- SEO content works because it can be changed and updated whenever you like.

- The copy that you write and that people respond to taps into the human condition – it works because you are relating to people on an emotional and needs based level. Harness this power.

- SEO copy provides for greater competition among industries and increases your ability to compete within that space – which in turn stirs the very motivation and passion in people.

- SEO content works because it provides for easy comparison between companies, products and services – which benefits your customers and prospects.

- SEO content works because it provides the means to expand your reach to new customers.

Chapter 3

ANALYZING YOUR WEBSITE'S COPY / USABILITY

How many websites have you seen that are confusing, hard to navigate or just plain bad? As someone who works on site copy and has writers who work on site copy, I see it everyday. Actually, *many* times a day. I think the majority of people out there just don't have the basics down when it comes to being able to write, and write for different mediums. Website design is a whole other story – that's even worse. It seems like we almost need an official design and guidelines standard that all websites would need to meet before they can be allowed on the web. Let's face it, a lot of web pages and web sites out there could use a little improvement in the copywriting department!

From boring prose to bad sentence structure, from poor logic to inadequate copy optimization, I've seen it all. And this is what your customers are reading as they jump on to your site! If they have to sludge through bad writing or long, drawn out writing, chances are they will get a negative feeling about your product or service. Is this the impression that you want them to have? Definitely not.

The bottom line is that bad copy means fewer sales. That's how important it is. Don't discount it. It's critical that this piece gets done right. One other point - an impressive site design can never rescue poor copy. There are lots of beautiful websites out there that have poorly written content. They usually end up being just that – a few pretty pictures. And forget about being found in the search rankings. It's not going to happen.

How to Approach Your Website Copy Analysis

How do you look at your site with a new set of eyes? What's the process that a copywriter goes through when they are rewriting a site? Good question. There are lots of different methods and approaches, but when you're trying to fix those broken sentences and phrases you should look at three areas separately:

- The Copy Itself - What's written?
- The Copy and how it relates to the design - How does it look on the page?
- Usability - Are you making it easy for visitors to find what they need?

The Copy Itself – What's Written?

The first thing to look at when you're analyzing a page of copy is the copy itself, naturally. That's the stuff that's staring you in the face when you log on to your site! So, how does it look? Really. Take a step back and seriously think to yourself, what would the average person think of this copy? Does it make sense to me? Would I understand what it is all about if I was on this site for the very first time? Remember when considering your site's web copy: People "scan" read – they don't take in every word. (We've covered that one.) And second, it's better comprehended when the copy is written the way people speak. Things have changed a lot for the written word over the last fifty years or so. There used to be much more structure and formality to writing. It was expected. There was also a strict adherence to grammatical "rules," like you can't end a sentence in a preposition or start with the word "and."

But you know what? That type of formal, cliché-ridden language is horrible to read! It's boring and uninteresting. It takes all the creativity away from people when you have to follow a set of strict rules. Did you know that some of the greatest composers of popular music can't actually *read* music? Paul McCartney is among them. He and his buddy John Lennon violated so many "rules" of music composition that it is really astonishing to think about. But you know what? That's what made their music *distinct*. They figured if it sounded good, then why not? Many of their songs have chords that are not even in the key of the song – but they work for all the right reasons. Well, it's the same thing with writing. Rules can get in the way.

Don't get me wrong. There are guidelines for the basic structure of copywriting on the web – that's what we're discussing in this chapter after all, but they don't handicap the expression of thought. They are merely the frame of the house, the words you write make up the rooms and truly make it a home.

So why not write the way people speak? It just makes more sense. It connects you with regular everyday people, some of whom didn't do that well in their high school English classes anyway! It doesn't mean you're less intelligent when you write this way – far from it. The very fact that you have a functioning website has already addressed that one.

Check out the way this book is written. If you take a look, you'll see many rules of grammar broken. And I'm a copywriter! Other professional writers say that same thing.

Using Bulleted Lists

One of the other important things to consider is the use of white space on your web pages. There needs to be some. A long, uninterrupted string of sentences that make up a massively long paragraph is the direct *opposite* of what we are looking for, but you see it on the web all the time. So, how can you break it up and get people's eyes to focus? Use bulleted lists. The copy can't be in standard block paragraphs like you see in books and magazines. Remember, you're competing for their time. If they don't get the information they need quickly, they'll jump to the next web site. If you use this formatting technique, it's probably a good idea to use it in the middle of the page. It looks more balanced in this position and can be used to communicate the most important information on the page, maybe the benefits that your customer will receive if they buy your product.

Numbered lists are great too, like a "top five uses for our product," or "top ten services we can assist you with." People's eyes are naturally drawn to these types of copy techniques. It's not just the domain of David Letterman!

Using bulleted lists may be the most underappreciated and underutilized formatting technique. It can really help communicate the copy. It's also good for your SEO effort.

With bulleted lists, you can turn this:

At Jackson-Peterson Consulting, we offer Smart Strategic Planning. Through this strategy we help develop clear, concise plans that match your team strengths and take advantage of opportunities. With Team Development Training, we help your company foster open communication and productive processes to facilitate interpersonal effectiveness and team synergy. Then there is our Executive Training program. With this offering, you'll be more effective, both with other executives and your employees, with our comprehensive consultation. We also offer Employee Development and Emerging Leader Consultation.

Into this:

Jackson-Peterson Consulting offers:

- **Smart Strategic Planning** - we help develop clear, concise plans that match your team strengths and take advantage of opportunities
    - **Team Development Training** - we help companies foster open communication and productive processes to facilitate interpersonal effectiveness and team synergy
    - **Executive Training** - you'll be more effective, both with other executives and your employees, with our comprehensive consultation
    - **Employee Development** - ensure your team has the skills and behaviors they need to do their jobs effectively
    - **Emerging Leader Consultation** - Natural born executives need key management and leadership skills to get to the next level

Your prospects are much more likely to notice it and read it when it's in this user friendly bulleted list!

The Quantity of Copy

Is there too much copy on the page? If you have more than 450 words per page, you have too much. Remember, people aren't reading for total literary absorption, they are seeking out key benefits or product attributes that can help them with a problem they may be facing. At the same time, you don't want too few words either. This, actually, is the more common offense. Having too little copy is pervasive on the web.

Those who utilize a simple seventy five-word paragraph may have good intentions; perhaps they feel that placing any more copy on the page would make it look cluttered. Or maybe they're trying to look cool or kitschy. You see tons of advertising agencies do this with their copy. No corporate speak here! They seem to take it to an extreme in trying to be cute or clever in their copy. They want you to know they're different, they are so *amazingly* creative, and you can see that now that you're reading this expertly crafted cute copy. But you know what? There's one problem with that. It is horrible for search engine optimization. Many of them may not care about that though, because they get most of their leads from referrals, not from unsolicited web searches. But, it illustrates the point. Make sure you have at least 200 words on the page and don't try to be too cute.

Then there is the often utilized, never-ending Home Page. You scroll and you scroll and you scroll. Where does the page end? This technique only works for those sometimes cheesy and very salesy direct response letters you see on certain sites and they only work sometimes. Most intelligent people don't buy into a direct response "online ad" type of offering. (more of this type of copy coming up.)

Is the Copy Interesting?

Does the copy grab you? Is it interesting and informative? Does it address your needs? And does the copy have a rhythm to it? It should. Is there variety in the writing? Are all the sentences long with multiple adjectives and adverbs? The goal is to combine short sentences with a few long ones. The trick is to make the copy flow. Using fragments is not a bad thing; quite the contrary actually. The occasional fragment or sentence that starts with

"But" or "And" can re-capture reader interest and keep it lively. Try it out. You'll like it. And your customers will too! (See how effective it is?)

Do this: go to a few of your favorite websites and try to remember what it was that you liked about them the first time you went to their site. Are you a part of their online community? Do you post comments to their blog? Do you simply like to buy from them? Or is it the way the copy reads that first captured you? Even though you may not have realized it, the copy probably was something that made you decide you liked it. But, it was a subconscious thing, so you probably didn't really think about it.

Are You Asking for the Sale?

What types of call to action are you using? Are you simply presenting information or are you trying to build a relationship with a customer? If your site is a "brochure" type of site where you aren't trying to sell anything, then it's probably alright if you aren't asking for the sale. But, the majority of sites out there do want the user to take some type of action.

So what do you have in the language that will make them do something? On your home page, you should have copy that motivates the visitor to go deeper into the site, such as "find out all the details of the special fall sale on the women's clothing page!" And then hyperlink "women's clothing" to that page.

Your product descriptions should have more than just features listed and an "Order Now" button. Get the benefits in there, up front. Let them know what else they receive if they buy right now, for example, "Get your choice of a free belt or handbag when you buy a dress today!" Compel them to take that next step! If you are trying to sign someone up for your newsletter list, do you just have the obligatory "Sign Up for our Newsletter" and a place for them to type in their email address? Or do you have some copy there that tells them why they should sign up and encourages them to do it?

Here's what we say on our site to encourage people to sign up:

"Receive two special reports including "The Future of Online Marketing" when you sign up for our free newsletter."

Using Headings and Subheadings

Like using bullets, headings and sub headings help break up the page and give the eye something to focus on. Your eyes need brief moments of rest as they scan read the article, they also need to take in specific information. Using headings and subheadings help make this process easier. The major purpose from a purely functional view is that they tell the reader what the page is about, and more specifically, what that section of the page is about. This is great for quick reviewing. If you are going from page to page on a site, seeking only information about a company's services, the headers can provide that information. Break up the page into digestible parts. Your customers will thank you for it with more sales.

In terms of what you want the words to say, we'll get to that in the next chapter. But one thing that bears repeating is this: keywords have an important place here.

AIDA
Attention
Interest
Desire
Action

AIDA

When you take a look at your site's copy, are you using AIDA? AIDA stands for: Attention, Interest, Desire, Action. Some have heard it before, maybe in a high school or college English class, but most people have not. Essentially, it's a style of writing that helps grab the reader's attention, build interest, and create a desire so they will take action, in that order. It reflects the way people like to be talked to. If you're selling something over the phone, the same order of steps apply. You really need to ask yourself, "Am I writing this copy for me and the way I like to write, or am I doing it for them, reflecting the way they respond to written words?" Ask yourself: Am I closing the deal with my customer? This is the ultimate goal of most copy. Make the reader do *something*. Fill out a survey, submit a request, sign up for a service, or buy the product. Whatever it is, you must have a call to action in the copy.

The Copy and How it Relates to the Design - How Does it look on the page?

What good would the copy be if it was placed on the page in long lines and block paragraphs?

Not too good.

Recently, I was working on a Home Page re-write for a financial services company that was having a conversion problem. They had no issue getting people to the site. They just couldn't make them buy once they got there.

After taking one look at their site, it was obvious. The copy was just thrown on the page with no variation in font sizes, font types, or eye appealing contrast. There was no customization to the site (it looked like they had used a website design template) and nothing to focus on. I think there was only one paragraph break in the 800 word Home Page manifesto.

Their competitor's Home Pages were very different. They all employed easy to read charts, testimonials, and other interesting design elements. My client had *none* of these. Obviously, something had to change, or his conversion rate would continue to suffer. Here are some of the things you want to look for when you consider the copy and how it relates to the design:

- Is there contrast in the type of fonts, the size of fonts, and the colors that are used? Some of the most eye-catching web sites use a few contrasting fonts, different sized fonts for the headers, sub headers and body copy, and a complimentary color palette. This approach wraps the content up into a great looking package and truly brings it to life. Here are two examples[16] of great copy immersed in brilliant design:
  http://www.6smarketing.com
  http://www.zephoria.com

- Is the copy broken up into readable/scanable sections? Or is it copied and pasted on the page haphazardly without regard to customer perception? Like my example above, you need to ensure the web page can be scanned in 30 seconds or less. Remember, we're dealing with short attention spans. In addition, studies have shown that it can be 20-30% more difficult to read from a screen than it is from print.

- Are the areas of the page that you want your customer's attention drawn to clearly visible? If you're using a "Learn More," "Buy Now" or other clickable button, is it obvious? Make sure it stands out on the page and can't be mistaken for something else. (By the way – don't use "Click Here." Its overused and looks amateur)

- Is the design simple and easy to navigate or is it cluttered? Some of the very best web sites are really very simple in appearance, even if they have lots of content. The rule here is to spread the copy out, having a unique page for every topic. Besides its obvious aesthetic reason, it's also great for SEO purposes. Don't "drown" your copy in a complex design structure or have a million different web pages on your menu. Remember, white space is important. Let the copy breathe!

Usability Analysis / Studies: Taking Your Website a Step Further

Much of what we have learned regarding website usability comes from researcher and writer Jakob Nielsen, Ph.D. He has been called "the best-known design and usability guru on the Internet" and the insight that we have gained through his studies have made a huge impact on how we improve the user experience. Almost all of the findings have a correlation to SEO copywriting, so it's important that we take a look at some of the key take-aways.

Probably one of the most fascinating findings has to do with *how people read on the web*. In Nielsen's groundbreaking eyetracking study from 2006, they recorded the reading behavior of 232 users[17.] By having them view thousands of Web pages, it was found that their reading behavior was pretty consistent. It didn't matter what the site or task was, there was a definite outcome. What did he find? That the dominant reading pattern looks somewhat like a large letter "F" on the page. His findings:

- Users first read in a horizontal movement, usually across the upper part of the content area, which formed the F's top bar.
- Next, users move down the page a bit and then read across in a second horizontal movement that typically covers a shorter area than the previous movement, which forms the F's lower bar.
- Finally, users scan the content's left side in a vertical movement. This last element forms the F's stem.

It should be noted that sometimes users read across a third part of the page content, making the pattern look more like an E than an F. Other times the reading pattern made it look like an inverted L. What are the implications for SEO copywriting? Place the most important copy in the areas where the eyes scan!

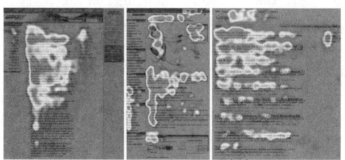

Heatmaps from user eyetracking studies of three websites. The areas where users looked the most are colored red; the yellow areas indicate fewer views, followed by the least-viewed blue areas. Gray areas didn't attract any fixations.

The above heatmaps show how users read three different types of Web pages:

- an article in the "about us" section of a corporate website (far left),
- a product page on an e-commerce site (center), and
- a search engine results page (SERP; far right).

Writing in the Style of Inverted Pyramids

Say what?

Let me explain... We know that people are scan reading your web pages. We also know that they are scanning it in interesting F and E patterns. So given these findings, how do we ensure that they get the information that you want to communicate? We do this by writing in the style of an inverted pyramid. What it means is put the most important information first, your major points. Follow this with supporting information and end with the least important details - background, maybe answer a couple of popular customer questions there, etc.

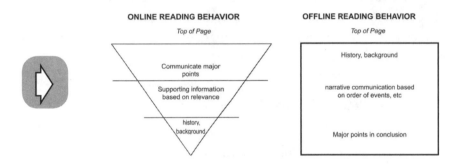

ONLINE READING BEHAVIOR

Top of Page

Communicate major points

Supporting information based on relevance

history, background

OFFLINE READING BEHAVIOR

Top of Page

History, background

narrative communication based on order of events, etc

Major points in conclusion

Easy Navigation - Make the Copy Simple to Follow

How many clicks does it take on average for your customers or prospects to find what they need on your site? Have you ever looked? Check out your website analytics program and see what the numbers are telling you. Follow their path from start to finish. This data is invaluable - and can help you re-design and/or rewrite if necessary. How many clicks should it take for them to get to what they are looking for? Probably less than five - but its less about the number of clicks and more about providing an intuitive, easy to follow path - no matter what they are trying to find.

Talk to your customers on this. See what they are telling you. Ask them point blank if they think your website is confusing. Is the copy and navigation holding them by the hand - or backing them into a corner? Get a handle on this, and you are a long ways towards making your site content rich!

Patterns, Alignment and Consistency

Take a look at each of your pages, individually and collectively. Do they have a consistent look and feel? Does the copy have the same tone and style? They absolutely need to. If you see major differences from page to page, this will not only look bad - it will throw your customers off and sometimes make them navigate to the next site. I know I have done it many times.

The other things you want to look at here are the locations of graphics, the site search box, menus, etc. There shouldn't be any variability with these site design elements. If you see problems here, you should seriously consider redesigning your site. If you notice that your copy needs a complete re-fresh as well, then this is a good time to do both. A total facelift - much easier than making design changes one year and copy changes the next!

Good Contrast Between Text and Background

Although this seems like an obvious usability point, you'd be surprised how many people are still not doing this step right.

Have you ever seen a website that had a black background and purple colored text? I have. How did a site like this get published? What were they thinking? Bottom line, if you can't see the copy clearly or have to squint to see it - its not working. A tried and true and very safe alternative? White background and black text. That's how most of the best sites are set up anyway. Your text and background choices are not a time to be creative; save that for the marketing materials or tag lines.

Strong Sentence Structure

If you don't know how to write an effective sentence, or struggle to put together a compelling and grammar balanced paragraph, you may want to leave the copywriting for someone who has a natural way with writing. Don't get me wrong, you can *learn* to write stronger sentences, but it's a process. Entire books have been dedicated to this topic, but our intention here isn't to go over the many details. Rather, we'll review the most important points for crafting good sentences.

First is to **keep your sentences simple**. If they are running five lines and have multiple prepositions and conjunctions, cut them up into digestible pieces. Remember, many people out there (probably 30-40%) are slow readers with remedial comprehension. You need to communicate at a sixth grade level so all potential prospects clearly understand. One thing about those slow readers: there's a ton of millionaires among them! And they may want to buy your product or service.

Next is **the word "you"**. Get used to using it! The copy on your website should be all about "you" (as in the customer, not you reading the book). "We want to help YOU find a better way to get from point A to point B and we want YOU to help us understand future product needs better". I think YOU get the idea!

Keep your paragraphs short. This helps people digest the information easier. Remember all those direct mail letters we used to get from Publishers Clearinghouse and all the others? (Actually we still get a lot of this stuff, right?) Recall how the letter would be structured? These letters would regularly have two to three sentence, sometimes only one sentence paragraphs. This helped break up the message and get unique points across. Same goes for your website. Long paragraphs scare people away. They don't have the time or inclination to want to read the whole thing. And they never will. Think simple.

Make your action in the verbs, not the nouns. If you are trying to get a point across, why not communicate it in the clearest, most direct way possible? You don't want to make prospects re-read your copy because they don't understand what you are trying to express. You want them to re-read it because they are thinking about buying from you! Here is an example of what I'm referring to:

Good verb

GOOD: The judge directly **explained** the verdict.

Noun hiding verb   bad verb

BAD: The judge's **explanations** for the verdict **were** direct.

Usability is an important element in the overall goal of making your site more attractive to prospects and customers. The copy that you place on your site supports its overall usability. Ensure that you go through the above steps one by one with each page on your site so you can take good advantage and be one step ahead of your competitors!

CHAPTER REVIEW

- The first step in analyzing your copy is to take a look at the words themselves – Make sure they connect with people and tell your story.

- White space is important on your web pages; be sure to use bullets and lists – it helps the copy breathe.

- If you have more than 450 words on a page, it's too much; shoot more for the 300-350 mark and you'll give your customers a better chance to digest what's on the page.

- Give the copy life – make it interesting, informative and enjoyable to read!

- Ask for the sale – use a strong call to action in your copy where appropriate.

- Definitely use headings and sub headings to help break up the page.

- Attention, Interest, Desire, Action – use these writing techniques, in this order, to get your prospect to take action.

- The design of the site needs to be balanced with the content – look at each page holistically.

- Website usability focuses on helping your visitors get what they need from your site, faster. Take advantage of these actionable recommendations to improve the user experience!

CHAPTER 4

KEYWORD RESEARCH – GETTING THE FIRST STEP RIGHT

Guess what? **Depending on the source, 50 - 70% of the people out there think that the companies listed at the top of the search engine rankings are the top companies in their field.** That's right – as high as 70%. I started off with this startling statistic because it has dramatic implications. It also talks to the power of keyword phrases and search engine optimized copywriting. You could be operating out of your den and be at the top of the search listings! And many online companies are doing just that. It keeps those fixed costs down, right? So, considering this impressive stat, here's what I did: I went to Google and did a very simple search. I looked for "sailboats." Typing in that one word keyword phrase and hitting enter, I had no idea what I would find. Although it's not the best example I've ever seen, it illustrates the point well.

So, here's what I found:

As suspected, there were four fairly well known, large sailboat manufacturers and/or distributors on the first page of results. They were in order: www.huntermarine.com, www.teamvanguard.com, www.seawardyachts.com, and www.macgregorsailboats.com. I didn't know a whole lot about sailboats, even though I've heard of a couple of them. Further investigation when I jumped on their sites proved that they are large, and entrenched. Some real quality companies. Then, as I scanned down the rest of the first page, I saw www.marinesource.com. It was the last listing on the first page, but it made it! Marine Source is a site that lists used sailboats for sale, boat shows, and has a great community element to it. Upon checking out the site and its copywriting, it clearly isn't in the same league as the ones mentioned above. But, the perception of the searcher is that it is! As you make your way through their site, you see that they definitely know what they are talking about and are providing a great service. The internal linking is great and the quantity of information is impressive. All in all, it's a great site. And you know what? There are probably fifty others just like it that show up on pages ten, fifteen, twenty three or even farther down the list. And those guys aren't getting the same amount of clicks. I guarantee it.

That's really a big part of what "branding" is all about on the web. Before the Internet came into existence, companies would try everything they could to build brand awareness. They would use expensive print ads, billboards, television commercials, radio and direct response sales letters. Anything to get their product in the mind of the customer through repetition, so that when the customer was ready to buy, they would think of that company.

Lots of consumers use the web to investigate before they buy, but at the same time, there are many people who are ready to buy when they log on. If you are on the first page of the search results for the keyword phrase they are using, and they click on your listing, they are definitely *aware* of you – and they more than likely will think you are a company that they would highly consider purchasing from.

So, being on that first page is kind of like having a well received television commercial, during prime time, in 1988, run over and over again. Of course, millions of people won't see you, but the ones that count will! Those that are searching for you! *Again, they are prequalified* – the odds are very good that they will purchase soon. So, the lesson here is if you do your SEO copywriting correctly and get your site optimized, you will go a long way to building your brand awareness.

So, what's stopping you from getting up higher on the list? Well, nothing is stopping you now. You have the bible of online copywriting, *Content Rich,* right here in your hands! Get started!

What are Potential Customers Using to Search for You?

Here's a "key" question: do you know which keyword phrases your customers are using to find you? Before you can answer, let me answer for you: No, you don't. You know why? Because there are literally hundreds (sometimes a few thousand) phrases that people could use to search for you. There are always more keyword phrases than you think. What's the best way to find out? Ask customers. They may not remember, but many will. That's very valuable information. Be sure you keep an ongoing log of what they tell you. I know for our clients, I always try to ask this question. Some of the responses I get are "seo copywriter," "web copywriting" or "website copywriter." But there have been others that surprised me.

So, that's the first thing you can do: it's easy and it doesn't cost you a thing.

Be aware too that keywords people use do change and evolve over time. They may be searching for plain Jane "sailboats" now, but when a new technology comes out, like let's say a 16 valve turbo engine, they may start using "turbo engine sailboats" too. Just be aware of what those keyword changes may be.

How can you get help in determining appropriate keyword phrases? I thought you'd never ask. This is the other very important step that you want to take. I mean, let's face it, the key to doing anything on the web, whether its help in the design aspect, determining the databases you want to use, or SEO copywriting, is finding the right organization to lean on, partner with and outsource to. Focus on your core competencies and find quality partners for the rest, right? Well, for the most part, you should know that you don't have to do that with SEO copywriting – you can do it yourself. But, you can also send the work out. So, back to the topic at hand: getting help with your keyword research.

The Help You Need: Word Tracker and Keyword Discovery[18]

For a subject as sophisticated and dynamic as Internet Keywords, we need all the help we can get. This is an art *and* a science, after all. Anything that combines those two disciplines is bound to be complex. The good news is that there are some great resources out there that deliver on their promise of comprehensive keyword analysis. Both of them charge a fee for full use of their service, but it is well worth the investment. The first of these is www.wordtracker.com. It's been around since 1999 and has been the de facto standard in the industry, highly recommended by all leading search marketing firms and top SEO copywriters.

As the "first mover" in the keyword analysis space, they came up with a unique way of looking at the words that we all use to find things on the World Wide Web. Although it's been eight years since they first came on the scene, they are still highly regarded and do a very good job for thousands of companies across the globe.

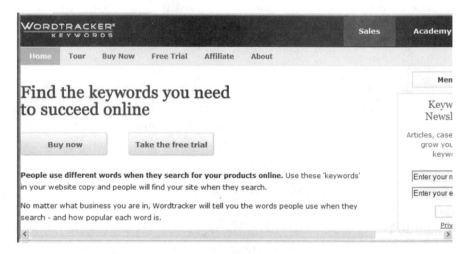

Their main claim to fame is what they call a "Keyword Effectiveness Index" (KEI) analysis. KEI is a formula that compares the popularity of a keyword phrase, which is the number of searches that contain the keyword phrase, to its usage popularity, which is the number of actual web pages it is found on. Although a little confusing at first, it does tell an interesting story. When you go to the site, you'll see that they offer a free trial. Do this. It's a great first exercise for any business looking to get a leg up on their online competitors. Or, if you just want to know more about how to optimize your website.

When you try it out, they'll ask you a few questions and go through a simple process of coming up with a target list of keywords. You'll see the "count" of each keyword. This is simply the number of searches performed for the keyword. You'll also see a KEI for each keyword phrase. Be sure to take some time analyzing what this is telling you. But don't put all of your faith in it. Wordtracker's KEI Analysis will tell you that certain keyword phrases are too competitive or popular and steer you away from using them. This isn't always the best advice.

Don't you want to be found for that super popular phrase? Of course you do. Sometimes it will take a while, but you may have to compete for that phrase and face your competitors head on. As we know, there are a lot of things you can do to further optimize your copywriting – (and your site) so that you can *own* that popular keyword phrase! Don't just give up and let your competitors beat you out.

Wordtracker can help determine how many competing sites are using the keywords you're looking at and can identify the phrases that have the greatest traffic potential. Some other things that Wordtracker can help you determine are keyword variations, word variants (example: dog tags vs. dog tag), and managing keyword lists. The cost to use their service is $329/year (As of June, 2008).

How does it get its information? Wordtracker regularly compiles a database of over 330 million search terms and is collected from Dogpile and Metacrawler. Why do they use these two and not Google or Yahoo? It's because many people use these two to check their rank for a keyword phrase, so it's not a totally accurate measurement of the keyword's popularity. Those that use Dogpile and Metacrawler don't really do keyword rank checking, so they work well for Wordtracker.

Of course, then the question becomes, do these searchers truly represent a good cross section of the population? Maybe, maybe not. The bottom line is it's a *good enough* gauge for the most part. If you want to try another, some say better, keyword phrase research tool, jump on to www.keyworddiscovery.com.

Keyword Discovery has been on the scene since 2004. It's also been adopted as the best keyword phrase analysis tool by many of the top search marketing industry gurus. At $49.95/month, it's more expensive than Wordtracker, but again, is well worth the investment. They do offer a free trial. Make sure you do it! How does it differ from Wordtracker? They use historical data from 32 billion searches from 180 search engines and use search logs from the engines as well. They also offer a year's worth of data so you can spot seasonal differences in keyword use. This can be valuable information, especially if you are a clothing retailer or have a cyclical type of online business.

If you are looking for a super robust tool, be sure to check out Keyword Discovery. Remember, uncovering only three or four important keyword phrases can alter the very landscape of your business – very quickly. This is as good as gold when it comes to your SEO copywriting effort. Utilize the power.

Free Keyword Research Tools

There are a few adequate keyword research tools that are free. These include Google Adwords Keyword Tool, Spy Fu (also has a paid option), SeoDigger, the SEO Book Keyword Tool [19] and Wordtracker's Free Keyword Analysis Tool.

With the Google tool, you don't get keyword demand. Rather, they show you an estimate of the number of clicks you may receive with an average bid. It does however support over 40 languages around the world, which appeals to an international audience, especially those interested in paid search.

The others mentioned above are all really cool and worth checking out – you can never have too much information on your keywords.

Analyzing Your Competitor's Keyword Phrases

This is something we have done ever since we opened our doors. If you want to increase your sales and improve your business, you've got to know what your competitors are doing, right? As you are making changes to your offering, so are they. Things are always moving, positions are always being jockeyed for; new markets are always in play. At the same time, they may

Web Site Home Page Source Code Sample

make some mistakes, as you could too. The nice thing about the web is that it lends itself very well to checking your competitors keyword phrases!

Just right click on the home page, select "view page source" and take a look at their Meta tags (source code), especially their title, description and keyword tags. If it's your first time doing it, you may be surprised how easy it is to acquire this information. You couldn't do this with your competitors in the pre-Internet days! In addition to checking their HTML code behind the scenes, you also want to be diligent in checking their inclusion of keyword phrases on their site. See where they appear and how often they use them.

A couple of things to keep in mind: your competitors don't always know what they are doing. They could be making the same mistakes as you with their keywords. Or, they could know exactly what they are doing. Are they checking you out? Assume they are, because it probably is the case. The other word of caution is to check more than just a couple of competitors. I would check most everyone on the first two pages for your most popular keyword phrases. It just makes sense to do a comprehensive job in this area. What you find out could be very interesting!

Do you Have a Site Search Box? Look at the Data Behind It!

Companies that have that little search box on their site – the one where you can type a word or two to find things that match those words on the site – have an ulterior motive. Yes, they want to help you find relevant information on the site. But, guess what? They also look at which words people type in that box for keyword research purposes! Knowing what and how they query can pay big dividends. I highly recommend you use this strategy on your own site.

Check Your Web Server Log Files!

Are you using WebTrends, ClickTracks 20 or some other log file analysis software? Mine it! This is great stuff to know. If you are new to this type of software, you should be aware that they can tell you which key phrases users typed into the search engines to find you. No guessing here, no asking them what they used to find you. Right there in the files will be all the search terms that were used. And this is just the tip of the iceberg with these types of software products. If you don't have one installed, seriously consider it. Another "well worth the investment" type of item.

Keyword Strategizing and Brainstorming

Talking to your management team about their keyword ideas is a great idea. Get everyone in a room and write them all out, have a lively discussion. One thing is for sure: the list will be longer than the one you wrote out. There are always hidden or forgotten keyword phrases that may be relevant. Next, you want to get into the strategizing part of the exercise. The first step here is to come up with a complete list of all the keyword nouns. Be sure to remember the basic breakdown: product category, segment of the market, brand names and individual model names.

An example of this would be "truck" (product category), "full size light duty" (segment of the market), "Ford" (brand name) and "F-150" (individual model names). Next would be looking at the corresponding adjectives for these nouns. And be sure to look at the full spectrum of adjectives, including comparison adjectives (tough light duty truck), qualifier adjectives (heaviest light duty truck), function adjectives (fastest light duty truck), attribute adjectives (2 ton light duty truck) and action adjectives (buy light duty truck).

Finally, think outside the box a little bit. Try and get inside your customer's head, maybe someone who has never bought a truck before and is totally new to the truck buying thing. What's going through their mind when they are getting ready to go online and perform a search? What problem are they trying to solve? What do they really want? What will they use in their search? Does the industry use certain jargon or clichés? If you call your product one thing and your customers call it something else, definitely be aware of this. This dynamic is a very common issue. Don't let it happen to you. Uncover the unknown.

Semantically Related Phrases

This is one step many companies miss altogether. What other words and phrases are similar to your main keyword phrases? Words have relationships to other words, and so when you think in terms of semantics, it could be as simple as the following:

- *auto, car, vehicle, motor vehicle and automobile.* These are all semantically related.

You could even take it a step further and look for words and phrases that look totally different, but are very much related. For example, with "SEO," it could be *search engine optimization, website promotion, online marketing, search, submission, high ranking, etc.* To see what related terms would be for your site, use the Google Keyword or Wordtracker tool.

How Popular Are Your Keyword Phrases?

Utilizing Google once again, I search for "cars." A very generic one word keyword phrase. At the very top right of the search, it says there are 356 million results for "cars." Wow – it would be tough to get ranked well for that keyword phrase, right? Yep. Really tough. Fairly impossible. And how many times was "cars" searched last month worldwide? 1.4 million times. Another humbling number. Next, I searched for "family camping tents." What did I find there? 1.5 million results, which would be much easier to rank for. If you sell tents and need to get a website up, there is hope! Last month this term was searched 6,500 times. Finally, to give you a full picture of the popularity or lack of popularity of keyword phrases, I typed in "Chesnik Kaleidoscopes." (I worked for the artist and owner of this business when I was 14.) The results there were a whole lot lower: only 822. Super easy to rank for that keyword phrase, but you wouldn't choose a phrase like that because it's the name of a business and their subsequent product, but you get the idea.

How does this concept apply to your company and your keyword phrases?

Aligning Keywords with the Customer Buying Cycle & Role Based Keyword Searches

This is a step that few companies ever take. Of course, we all know that not everyone who jumps on the web is going to buy the very first time. They really are doing one of four things: gathering information, trying to learn about the product/service, shopping, or buying. The key thing to know is that for each point in the buying cycle, they have a likelihood of using a unique type of keyword phrase. For example, if we were talking about buying a car, a keyword phrase they may use in the education step would be "2007 Best Cars." At the shopping stage, they may use "car dealerships in Atlanta." At the buying stage, they may use still another unique keyword phrase, like "Toyota Camry in Atlanta" or go back to the dealership's site and buy a car right off their website. Be aware of the customer buying process when you optimize your site's copywriting.

Role-based keyword searching behavior is another interesting SEO dynamic. Basically, it breaks down to this: who is searching – the president of the company, the market research guy or the sales person? For example, what do they use as their keyword phrase and why? You need to align your keyword phrases with the type of people who are seeking you out – if possible. Some websites even categorize their product pages by customer role; it just depends on your specific customer set. This concept is worthy of mentioning because it may be a great opportunity for you to write more targeted and specific pages tailored directly for a particular type of customer set.

Look for Emerging Keyword Phrases

We live in a super fast, turbo-charged Web 2.0 world. Things are changing all the time. Your competitors are moving – some of them very quickly, to dominate your business. Online, they are going to be coming after you fast on the keyword phrase front. Ask yourself this question: What are my customers searching for *today* to try to find me? That's the million dollar question. You'll find that keyword searching evolves over time and new trends can influence the process. What your prospects typed in the Google search box one day can be different on the next.

So, what are the *emerging* keyword phrases for your industry? Stay on top of your competitor's source code and site copy to see what they are using, and then use your due diligence on Word Tracker and Keyword Discovery to see what the latest is. I know for my business, "online copywriting" has come to be a much more popular keyword phrase than it ever was before. Others, like "freelance copywriting" haven't done as well. So, like everything, it's a moving target. You'll need to optimize your copy based on these new emerging keyword phrases.

Don't let your competitors do it first!

Keyword Analysis – Which Ones Lead to Conversions?

Good question! Check your site analytics program, logs and ask your customers. Information is power.

Keyword Nuances – Some Other Important Considerations

Be aware of these often overlooked keyword research issues:

- Multiple audiences: a certain keyword phrase may apply to two totally different industries or purposes ("policing" – could be "policing the community" or "policing the Internet")

- Related meanings: Avoid a broader term (warranties) when a more specific one will do (home warranties).

- Acronyms: Beware of double meanings in your keywords.

- Plural/singular issues: "trucks" and "truck" – there are differences.

- Multiple intents: "Hotel" and "Lodging" – they may mean the same thing to you, but the term "hotel" will have a higher conversion rate.

CHAPTER REVIEW

- Know which keyword phrases your customers are using to find you.

- Wordtracker and Keyword Discovery are some of the best tools out there for keyword research – be sure to check them out.

- There are quite a few free keyword research tools available too, don't let something so valuable go unused.

- Analyze your competitor's keyword phrases by checking their page source code and reading their pages.

- Check your web log files – lots of hidden information resides here.

- Talk to others in your company about keywords, brainstorm a large list and then begin eliminating as necessary.

- Determine how popular your keyword phrases are and see if there are opportunities to match them up with buying cycles.

So, now that you know which keywords you want to use, how do you place them in your website copy? Good question... let's get right into that. Time to optimize!

CHAPTER 5

OPTIMIZING YOUR SITE CONTENT

This is probably the most important chapter in the book. As such, it will probably be the longest. But, rest assured, you're going to get a ton of great information here that you can start implementing right away, so strap yourself in and get ready. Here we go!

The first thing to remember is that you are doing two things at once: **writing for the search engines and writing for your customers.** Google is looking for certain things on your site that humans are not – that's just the plain and simple truth. But how are they different? How do you write for both at the same time? Why do we have to be concerned? These are all questions that we will answer.

 Know that if you are looking for one golden rule of content writing on the web, it is this: *write for people first, search engines second.*

So, let's understand a bit how the search engines work exactly.

SEARCH ENGINE CONSIDERATIONS

Filtering and Ranking

The search engines – Google, Yahoo, MSN and all the rest are huge players in the overall Internet industry. Everything they do impacts the web in big ways. Ten years ago, they were practically non-existent. Today, they are not only the key movers and shakers of the World Wide Web – they are giant multi-national companies that wield great power. So what do you need to know to understand how to work with the search engines? How do they set the rules for the way the game is played?

Well, first, of course is to get your site <u>ranked</u>. This can be a challenge if you're just starting out. I remember when I first launched my site way back when – not really understanding SEO at the time. My site designer didn't know much about the optimization process either. So, as such, my site wasn't optimized and because I didn't use keyword phrases in my copy, it didn't rank. At all. I would search over and over again, week after week and wonder why my site wouldn't come up. I finally woke up one day, discovered search engine optimization and changed my entire strategy. I rewrote my site copy, changed designers and came out with a totally new site. Within a few weeks, I was ranking for "seo copywriting," "website copywriter" and others. Once your site is indexed by Google and Yahoo, you are <u>in the game</u>. What is the criteria they use to make the decision on which sites get placed where? They do this by using *filtering and ranking*.

With Filtering, search engines decide which pages are in the search results and which are not. If you meet their criteria, you will be filtered into the results. This topic is fairly easy to understand and as such, we won't spend much time discussing it. Essentially, the search engines filter by language, character, and country. They also filter by picture, image, presentation, etc. If you are writing English content for your website, you don't have to be too concerned with filtering.

With Ranking, search engines search results by relevance to decide which pages get to be at the top of the list. Because ranking issues are so important when it comes to SEO copywriting, this is the area we'll discuss the most.

The Ranking Algorithm and All that Goes With It

Without getting into too much detail, a search engine algorithm is a complex mathematical formula that determines how web pages are ranked. So if you have a site that sells hand bags and "hand bags" is the keyword phrase, how does Google's ranking algorithm deal with it? Well, it will look at all the indexed pages for the phrase "hand bags" and determine which pages are the most relevant or "important" for that phrase. The ones that are the most relevant will end up on the first page of the search results.

What factors go into the algorithm? That's a closely guarded secret within the hallowed halls of Google corporate headquarters. And it changes all the time.

There are probably over 100 factors that go into the final equation. Most of them, you don't have to worry about – you wouldn't know what they are anyway. But, there are many well known factors that you can directly influence through the power of SEO copywriting on your site.

Factors that Help Your Page Rank Well

Google's "PageRank" is the most well known page factor. If you aren't aware of it, it's the little horizontal bar on the Google Toolbar that displays a web page's importance – shown by a strength indicator in the bar that ranks from 1-10. A score of ten would be a very important site, a score of 0 would be totally unimportant. A page that has good PageRank would have a five or six score. A site like Yahoo or Amazon would have a score of ten. By definition, "page" factors consider anything the search engine knows about the page, the site and the other sites that link to that page.

Without getting into too much non-copywriting search engine optimization information, the most important page ranking factors are link popularity, popularity data that the search engines extract from your computer (for those who have the Google or Yahoo toolbar installed), URL length and depth, how often your page is updated with new information, and organized, structured web design. Now that you know these, let's get into the specific content related factors that your focus on copywriting will help.

The Query Ranking Factor

Why is it called the query ranking factor? Because the search or "query" that someone types into Google determines what pages come up. You in turn can do certain things on your page with the copy to make sure your page is ranked high. The most important and most basic thing to understand? *The keyword phrase has to be used on your page in order for the page to rank*. Most people understand this concept, but it's still important to spell it out once more.

So what are all the other query factors that play an important part in your site copy?

Keyword Frequency

Keyword frequency used to be the most important or *one* of the most important factors. What is it? It's the number of times your keyword phrase occurs on the page. Typically, you are looking for the keyword phrase to be used at least three times throughout the page (assuming you're not writing 600 words or more). You'll probably have a couple more keyword phrases that you'll want to use too, so if you have a total of three keyword phrases that makes nine places that you'll be using your phrases on a certain page. On the other side of the equation, don't use your keyword too frequently – that's called *keyword spamming*. Not only is it a bad idea, but people reading the copy will be turned off and worse yet - it could get you banned from the search engines.

One little secret – and this is something you don't hear about often: you don't always have to repeat the exact phrase time after time throughout the copy. You simply need to use the words that make up the phrase as many times as necessary throughout the page. What do I mean? If your keyword phrase is "portable poker tables," you need to repeat the word "portable" three times, "poker" three times, and "tables" three times. These occurrences can realistically happen anywhere on the page – but just know that there are better places than others, more on that in a bit. One caveat however: the goal should be to use the complete phrase as it is written, but you can do it this other way as well and still get search engine ranking benefits.

To give you an example of how keyword frequency is used on a real site, let's consider a project I did for www.CrowleyMarine.com.21 This company sells all kinds of boats and boat engine parts. One of the pages I wrote for them was about Stern Drives. The keyword phrase that they wanted to use was "Mercruiser Stern Drives." Their current page only used it once – not enough to get ranked very high for that phrase. On the new page, I placed it in the page header "Mercruiser and OMC Stern Drives," towards the end of the page with the sentence "Whatever your Mercruiser or OMC Sterndrive needs may be, we have the exact part in stock and ready for delivery" and as a separate sub header at the bottom of the page. Here's how the new page looked:

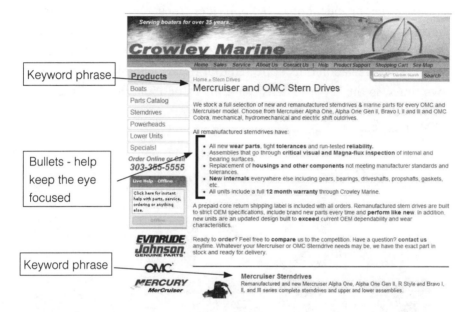

Keyword Density

So, taking it a step further, let's consider keyword density. The density is the percentage of the total words on the page divided by the number of times the keyword phrase appears. What do the search engines look for on keyword density? Between 3-8%. So, if you have 350 words on the page, you'll want each word of the keyword phrases to add up to 18-25 total occurrences. When working with your keywords in the copy, make sure all those keyword phrases are spaced out well. You don't want it to look obvious. Remember, you want your copy to be read like the prospective customer is having a conversation with you. You definitely wouldn't tell someone the following: *"Bob, we sell decorative Christmas wreaths that are guaranteed to last 30 years or more; our Christmas wreaths are made from the finest materials and our Christmas wreaths are shipped to your door within two days. Would you like to buy one of our Christmas wreaths?"*

I think you get the point.

To give you an example of how keyword density is used on a real site, let's consider a project I did for www.CaliforniaDreamin.com, a local company that provides hot air balloon rides. Their keyword phrases for the home page were "hot air balloon ride" and "bi-plane ride." After re-writing their content, the total number of words on the page was 205 - a little light. "Hot air balloon ride" appeared four times and biplane ride appeared two times, so the keyword density is 20/215 or about 9% - a little on the high side, but not too high.

Here's how the page appears:

Keyword Prominence

Just like the military, there's a hierarchy, a rank and order for the words that appear on any given web page. Certain placing of words makes no difference to the overall search engine algorithm. Other places are very important. Where is the most important or most prominent place for an important keyword phrase? The first word of the page's title, or header. The search engines consider this an important place on the page, because it's a great indicator for what the page is actually about. So, titles, headers and sub headers are perfect places for keywords. They will be very prominent in these positions. Not only will the search engines see them, but people will too.

Another good place on the page is at the very end. You'll also want to scatter them a few places throughout the body text, but just realize that this isn't a very prominent place to put them.

To give you an example of how keyword prominence is used on a real site, let's consider a project I did for www.batterystuff.com. The keyword phrase was "motorcycle battery." You can see that I placed the phrase in the first header and sub-headers. I also placed it in the body copy a few times, but the headers (and the end) are two very prominent locations. Here it is:

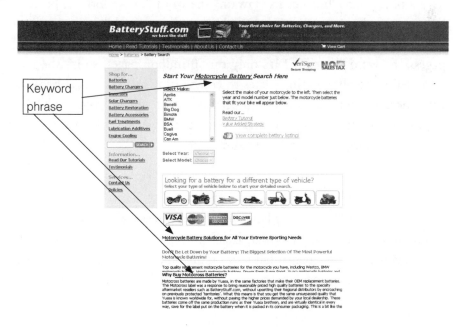

Aligning with the Searcher's Intent

If you search for an "ipod product guide," you'll probably get a PDF document in the search results. This is Google trying to match the results with what you intended to find. People search for a variety of reasons, but if you were to break it down to the most essential reasons they would be:

- They search for information
- They search to purchase and perform a transaction
- They search to navigate, trying to find the home page of a certain site

You want to try to match your intention for a particular page with the searcher's intention. This can be done very easily if you write the copy with the searcher in mind.

As time goes on, there will be more and more of this type of personalization and customization with the search engines.

Keyword Term Rarity

This simply refers to the fact that keyword phrases have certain words that are important and more rare than other words within the phrase. If you have a phrase like "beaches in Hawaii," the word "in" would not be very important and not very rare. The word is actually on 6.6 billion web pages! The word "Hawaii" is on 170 million - so more rare, but still a ton of pages. The word "beaches"? It's only on 50 million pages, so it's the rarest word in the phrase. This relates to copywriting for your pages because you'll need to understand keyword phraseology if you are going to be using this important concept to maximum advantage. It's one of the lesser important concepts, but still worth knowing.

Keyword Term Proximity

If you search for "beaches in Hawaii," the best pages are probably going to be those results that show that exact phrase in that specific order. Of course, you'll get some pages that focus more on beaches than Hawaii, and you'll get some that focus more on Hawaii than beaches, but the goal is to get pages that focus on both - and do a really good job explaining what beaches are like on the Hawaiian Islands. Maybe a site or two that rates them, talks about their history and explains what the waves are like there.

So, "proximity" simply means how close each of the keywords are to each other on the results pages when you search. In doing a quick test, I ran the search on Google and found out that the top website in the natural search listings was www.bestplaceshawaii.com 22 and the page title was "10 Best Beaches in Hawaii" - a great result for the search! Pretty much exactly what I was expecting. Incidentally, the keyword phrase "beaches in Hawaii" was all over the page - in all the right places. Consider that a lesson learned!

WRITING FOR PEOPLE

The Goal: Conversion

Now that we've exhausted the topic of what the search engines are looking for and how they "read" the page, it's time to turn to the subject that's most important in optimizing your page: how you write for your customers - future or current. Like a brochure, you are putting your website out there for people to read - but more than that, you are trying to convince them to do business with you, or at least pique their interest so they'll want to find out more. The words you use (and the way they look on the page and integrate with the design) can make this happen. Your goal? To convert that person from someone who knows nothing about your company to a full fledged, paying customer. Whether you consider that conversion to be signing up for a newsletter, downloading a white paper, buying something on the site or simply contacting the company for more information, it all comes down to one thing: you want that person to take action!

Plus, you can't pretend to know how to control or predict what the search engines are going to do - don't be concerned about Google's forever changing algorithm. You can't possibly alter your page to always please the search engines. Sometimes, your Products page may fall to the second results page and you'll wonder why. As long as you are writing with people in mind first and doing all the right things as it pertains to the search en-gines, you'll be fine. So, what is the process for optimizing a certain page? Let's take a look.

The Process for Page Optimization

The basic process for page optimization is this: choose your page, write the copy, analyze how the page is performing and then improve the page if necessary. If you continue to be unsatisfied with how it is doing, just keep tweaking it until you have what you want. Of course, you'll need to put it in perspective. If you are going up against some tough competition with a popular keyword phrase, you may never get to the first page of the search engine results. You need to be realistic. It can be a frustrating process, but one that could provide great rewards. It took me a long time (many months) to get to the top spot on Google for "website copywriting," but once I did, it was a great feeling. For all the business we get, it still is the number one source for our largest jobs.

Deciding on a Page to Optimize

How do you start? Look at your keyword phrases. You probably have a list of at least twenty. If you are a large company with many products or services, you could have hundreds. You'll have general keyword phrases and more specific phrases. You'll see phrases that seem like they would go together, and some that are more popular than others. If you are opti-mizing the home page for a watch retailer, you'll optimize for "watches," "watch accessories" and "watches for sale." If you are writing the products page, you'll optimize for "Rolex watches," "Tag Heuer watches" and "Bre-itling watches" for example. Some keyword phrases will appear on multiple pages. If you are an exclusive Rolex watch retailer, "Rolex watches" could appear on the home page *and* the products page.

There will always be a phrase or two that won't seem to fit on any page - just because the phrase came though as a possible good one during the keyword research process does not mean you have to use it. One thing you can do is search for that phrase on Google and see how other sites are using it; this may help get the ideas flowing.

If you can't find a way to make it fit, then don't force it. If you can create a new page, however, and find enough to write about around that phrase, then definitely do it! You could generate new traffic to your website in a very short amount of time.

One of the goals is to match a set of keyword phrases to what that page is specifically about – so if you are a fish market and you have a product page on shellfish, you want to use the same – themed keyword phrases of "fresh lobster," "soft shell crab" and "fresh ocean shellfish" all on that page. The more general keyword phrase "San Diego fish market," for contrast purposes, would go on the home page.

Making Three Keyword Phrases Work All in the Same Sentence!

Another little secret – you can make four separate keyword phrases all work in the same sentence. Here they are:

- Paint supplies
- Artist brushes
- Oil based paint
- Art supplies

And our sentence:
Buy oil based paint and artist brushes at Art Supplies.com

Isn't that great? It works beautifully.
Note: you don't have to repeat the same word in the sentence if it appears in two unique keyword phrases.

Keyword Extensions / Building Out More Pages

If you want to really give your keywords power and you have lots of one type of item, like cosmetics for example (and you are a retailer of all types of beauty products), be sure to build out additional pages to support all the various sub-sections of a keyword group. Here would be an example list of keywords:

- Facial cosmetics
- Cosmetics for teens
- Women's cosmetics
- Men's cosmetics
- Organic cosmetics
- Hypoallergenic cosmetics

All you need to do is build a unique page for each and then on the facial cosmetics page for example, use even more specific keyword phrases within that phrase, such as "facial cleansing cosmetics," "facial exfoliating cosmetics," etc. *It's all about starting from the very general keyword phrases (reserved for your doorway or entry pages (like Home, and Products) and then getting more and more specific with the keyword phrases as you work your way down the site navigation layers.*

A Great Example: How I Improved one Client's Landing Page

First things first: search for a few of the keyword phrases you want the page to rank for and see what turns up. At the top right, you'll see how many competing pages you have worldwide for that phrase. If it's over a million, you know you have a lot of work to do; it's going to be competitive ranking well for that phrase. You'll also want to see who your competitors are for that keyword phrase. Are they big companies with well known brand names? Are they small mom and pop websites? Or is it a little bit of both?

Click on a few and see how they are using the keyword phrase and how their site looks. After you do this simple exercise, you'll know what you're up against as you start to write (or in this case *edit*) the page.

In looking at the great art of improving an existing web page, you are faced with the following dilemma: do I change a little here and there and try to work around what they have, or do I start from scratch? Usually, it's somewhere in between. The benefit of having some existing content on the page is that it will help you get the thought process started and assist in generating some ideas.

I had a client approach me four months ago with a web site editing project. The website was www.catchquick.com, 23 a shopping search engine. The problem with the site copy was that it was written by someone who didn't have a firm understanding of the English language; actually I believe the client was from Europe, operating in the U.S. So, from a copy standpoint, there were obvious grammar problems and sentence structure issues. But, the existing content didn't communicate anything on what the site was actually about; it was more a short essay on the frustrations of trying to find what you are searching for on the web.

We did some keyword research for the site and discovered that "shopping search engine," "online coupon codes" and "discount coupons" were all very good keyword phrases that applied to what the site offered. So, we built the home page around these terms. We also gave the content a good benefit story, proper flow, a nice sense of contrast in the language and a strong call to action. Finally, we doubled the word count and used a bulleted list in the middle to help the eyes focus better on the page.

Here's the before and after images of the page:

BEFORE:

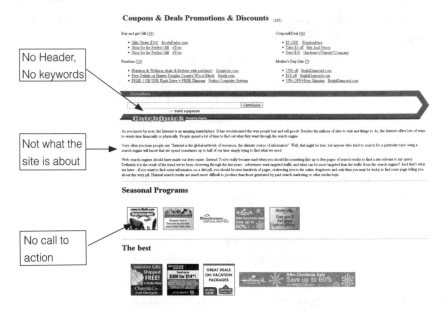

No Header, No keywords

Not what the site is about

No call to action

AFTER:

Buy and get Gift (49)

- Shop for the Perfect Gift   eToys
- Over 1,300 GIFT IDEAS That Give ALL YEAR Long.   MAGAZINES.com
- Omaha Steaks Gift Cards!   OmahaSteaks.com

Freebies (62)

- Skin-So-Soft Bug Guard Plus: Buy 1 Get 1 FREE!   AVON
- Golf Digest Bonus. Free 12 month subscription with purchase of $25 or more at 3balls.com   3balls Golf
- Free Promgirl E-book with membership!   Promgirl!

Coupon&Deal (35)

- Save 25% off   CODi
- Get 6% off   Scented Monkey
- Save $10   Gardener's Supply Company

CatchQuick Promotion (145)

- Honolulu Hotels - up to 60% off!   EasyClickTravel.com
- Up to 50%   HearthSong
- FREE Shipping   MenScience

CatchQuick: The Easiest Shopping Search Engine on the Web!

Welcome to CatchQuick, the easiest and most user friendly **shopping search engine** in the world. Here you can find the best stores, coupons, deals and promotions across the web, all organized on our site for easy ordering. When you search a web store on your own, it can be difficult to find their discounted offerings. Sometimes, they can even be hidden. Now, all you have to do is come to CatchQuick. We do all the work for you - we find the very best deals and pass them on to you!

The Internet is the world's greatest marketplace. It has revolutionized the way people buy and sell goods and services. It has transformed the way we interact with one another and the way we live. With all the millions of sites to visit and online activities we can spend our time pursuing, the challenge really becomes *finding what we want*, especially when it comes to shopping and locating online deals. CatchQuick makes it easy. Simply log on and click away! Your favorite web store, gift idea or discount coupons are all right here.

A Large Selection of Online Coupon Codes, Deals, and Unique Gift Ideas

Search engines make our lives easier. But *shopping* search engines make our lives more fun! Here is just a small sample of some of the great benefits you'll enjoy when you use CatchQuick:

- The newest and best online stores
- Organized by product, gift type, and type of store
- Gift ideas for every occasion
- Coupon offerings featuring deals up to 50% off
- Save time and money!

Discount Coupons and Daily Freebies

Don't forget our incredible discount coupons and daily freebies! Everything you could want, from seasonal programs to the most

Headers and Sub headers – Make them Snappy

You can see in the prior example that we followed a certain strategy in regards to the headers. For the first one, "Catchquick: The Easiest Shopping Search Engine on the Web!," we used the company name, Catchquick, the most important keyword phrase - Shopping Search Engine and communicated a good benefit - it's the easiest on the web. Many times, we use the company name for the first header. It helps brand the site and positions the name so it will be remembered. Its also good if the site name or company name is unknown. You wouldn't do it for Marriott or Hershey's, but you would for "Huntington Vacations" or "Dynastar Productions."

For the second header, "A Large Selection of Online Coupon Codes, Deals and Unique Gift Ideas," we brought up an additional service offer that clearly communicated you could get a great deal by using this website. We also snuck in two other important keyword phrases: "online coupon codes" and "online deals." The fact that "online" is there only once is fine, they could get ranked for both keyword phrases regardless. Finally, on the last header we used "Discount Coupons and Daily Freebies," which were the other phrases that came up as important, but not as important as the others. We also changed their meta tag copy to match.

Unfortunately, "shopping search engine" is a very popular phrase with 81 million sites competing, but their page is still a whole lot better than it was and now they are at least in the game.

The key with headers is to make them short, snappy, and memorable. You'll also want to use your keyword phrases and bring up a benefit if possible. If you can do all that, you are doing well.

Body Text – Conversational and Convincing

The body text makes up the majority of the page. As such, it's very important to get right. The biggest problem with most home pages out there? Not enough words on the page. Second biggest problem? Not using the right (or any) keywords. The point with the body copy is to really bring the reader into the page, get them interested and eager to know more. You want the language to be conversational, as we discussed in a previous chapter, but more than this, it needs to have a rhythm and a flow. If you have three paragraphs or sections, each one should stand alone. They shouldn't all be saying the same thing.

The way I do it is this: if I have three keyword phrases and three paragraphs to use them in, I'll make each keyword a focus in each paragraph. Of course, I'll use each keyword phrase a second and third time in the other paragraphs, but each section could be used to highlight a specific keyword phrase. This is a great way to break them up and make sure you are spacing them out the way they should be.

Definitely take the time to look at how your competitors are building their pages too. This will show you what not to do on your pages as well as what *to do*. If a competitor who is selling the same exact product as you has a poorly written body section with no comparison to other similar products, make sure you include a competitive feature/benefit diagram like this on your site!

Bold, Italicized and Linked Keywords

Have you been on a site and seen that some of the words are bolded, italicized and/or hyperlinked? All of these actions help a little bit because the words stand out to visitors, which in turn motivate the search engines to give them more consideration too. So what's the strategy here? Do it to a few of your keyword phrases or other important words. You don't want to bold or italicize too many words, otherwise they won't stand out. In terms of internal linking those words, only do this if those words naturally would refer to other pages, like if you were a watch retailer and mentioned Rolex watches, you would want to hyperlink the words "Rolex watches" to the product page that discussed them in detail. For more information on linking, reference a good book on overall Search Engine Optimization, we list a couple in the Appendix.

The Call to Action

We talk about how to write good call to action copy in another chapter, but it's worth mentioning here too because typically your call to action will come towards the end of the page, which is a great place for keyword phrases too.

Here's how we do it on our home page. Notice how we include the keyword "copywriting":

"What's our secret? Conversational, keyword-rich **copywriting** *that persuades with power and conviction. What drives us? A passion for writing and search marketing. We think you'll be passionate about what we can write for your business. Get in touch today! (760) 451-8700"*

Putting it All Together – Harmonizing Your Content

So when you finish writing the page, how do you ensure everything looks good, sounds good and generally "works"? We'll get to web/copy analysis in just a couple pages, but at this point you basically want to step away, print out what you have and look at the copy *holistically.* Performing all the separate pieces is one thing - making sure you write about product or service benefits, including a good header or two, implementing keywords, but how does it *all fit together?* You'll want to have others read it and get their opinions. That's a good idea no matter what you write, print items included. But for yourself, you'll want to be able to take an assessment of the copy and audit the words you've put together so you can do it with everything you write. You can't always rely on others to give you feedback.

So, what are some simple little rules to remember as you write so you can *harmonize the content while you are writing it?*

First, use variety in the language. Use a simple sentence followed by a more complex one, followed by a fragment, or some other unique combination. What you are trying to get away from is boring, uniform copy. Utilizing *contrast* is a good idea, it makes things stand out. By making the sentence structure varied, you make it interesting. By making it interesting you provide good contrast. By giving your copy a good dose of contrast, you motivate people to buy. See how I did that? Look at the last three sentences I wrote and you'll get an idea of how to implement some style, contrast and interest to your words!

You also want a unified thought process so the entire section of copy has a good rhythm and flow to it. If you feel like you are rambling with the content, you probably are. Make every sentence count. One of the rules of songwriting is to make every word in the lyric count – writing content for the web is really no different. All the while you are doing these things, be looking for link opportunities; you want to use linking on some of your keyword phrases – both internal and external linking. If you are a retailer who does most of their business in the community where you are located, you'll also want to be thinking "local" on the language you choose and keywords you use. Place the most important information, the feature/benefit story right up front near the top. Wherever people start reading is the perfect spot for the information you want them to remember.

Another writing technique you can use is *alliteration*, which is using the same letter or sound of the letter repeatedly in a sentence. Something like this maybe:

Atlanta's Awesome Announcements for August.

Using alliteration can grab instant attention from your reader. Another tool just as effective is *repetition*. You can use this very effectively in a 4-5 line section. Maybe something like this:

America is in need of true and distinguished leadership.
America has long been the beacon of liberty and truth.
America needs your help in the quest for a better future.
The time for America – is now.

One other technique that my 10th grade English teacher said over and over again way back in high school was this: *"Be sure to show, don't tell, in your essays!"* Using this little treasure can be difficult for a lot of people, because so many spend their lives talking – and writing in the "telling" kind of way. How does this work exactly? Try this on for size:

Telling: The vegetable soup tastes amazing; it's the best soup I've ever had!

Showing: *The aroma of garden fresh mushrooms and thyme was only out done by the taste of the soup's warmth swirling in my mouth. I ate it like a hungry bear and went back for more – twice.*

Use *positive language*. Instead of pointing out why they shouldn't buy the competitor's product, focus on why they *should buy* yours. Use engaging, positive language instead of double negatives as you describe your service. An example of what not to do:

There is nothing worse than a kitchen appliance that doesn't work; stay away from Millers kitchen mixers – unlike ours, they provide less than adequate power and are unreliable over a long period of time.

Something else you could do – and this is a recommendation you don't hear very often is to study the masters of writing – some of the best copywriters, like Bob Bly and others as well as some of the better direct marketers out there like Joe Sugarman 24. Although I'm not a huge fan of the direct response copy technique on the web, I know it can be effective for certain audiences and specific products and services. Every time I read one of those long sales letters with testimonials sprinkled throughout and multiple calls to action, I think, "Who falls for this stuff?" It's crazy. But I know that many do. Different people respond differently, right? With direct marketing copy techniques, I am referring to more the title tag, snippet (discussing next) and then your main text on the page. You want to use copy that "leads" the prospect to the eventual call to action. The title and snippet are what appear on the search engine results page and gives them a taste of what's to come.

Finally, to harmonize content, you want to always be thinking "keywords." Look for those general nouns like balloons, cars and rings and think – is there a more descriptive way to describe them, maybe a way that incorporates a keyword or two? There always are. How about "hot air" balloons, "formula one race" cars and "diamond solitaire engagement" rings? Presto, you've just used your keyword phrases, now do it again and again (But not too many times).

Doing all these things at once is something that will take time to do; writing after all is something you can learn. And some people won't be able to do all of them at once. Your style may be to take them one at a time. That's fine too. What you are trying to do with all these techniques is ***find your voice.*** Once you have it, you'll be able to use it time and time again – on anything you write for the web. Different products, services, companies and divisions require different types of copy, but your style can remain consistent throughout.

Meta Tag Copy

Meta tags are one of the most misunderstood parts of the search marketing and SEO copywriting process. For the sake of clear understanding, we're going to make it very simple. First, what are they? Meta tags are code that is found both in the html pages of your site architecture AND what you see displayed on the page when you do a search. There are two important ones: The Title tag and the Description tag. The title tag uses 2-3 keyword phrases and/or benefits to tell the searcher what the page is about. It needs to read almost like a headline – this will motivate people to click on it. If you are thinking about using your company name in the title, it's probably a good idea *not to*; this is valuable real estate. Are people searching under your company name anyway? Most likely not.

The description tag takes it one step further and explains in a little more detail about that page and what the company is offering. Two important points on Meta tags: every page needs to have unique tags, with unique keyword phrases (generally true on the phrases) and you want to write them with the idea that you are trying to "sell" that person on clicking on your site to find out more. Basically, it's a little ad that is out there on the web, bringing your clients in. Many times, it's the first thing people see about your site, so you want to make sure they are right!

Here is something you should do right now: jump on to Google and type in "site:www.your domain.com" – fill in *your domain* with whatever your site URL is. What pops up are all your titles and descriptions for pages indexed by Google. Are they all the same? That needs to change! Every page needs unique titles and descriptions.

To illustrate the use of Meta tags further, here are the home page Meta tags from my site and what actually displays in Google and Yahoo for that page:

Home page:

META TAGS

<title>Website Copywriting | SEO Copywriter | Freelance Copywriting</title>
<meta name= "**description**" content="Custom Copywriting is the number one source for all of your SEO web copywriting needs. We are the fastest growing web copywriter in the nation because we provide superior copywriting that persuades with power and conviction. Utilize our freelance copywriter expertise to improve your online sales.">

Yahoo:
Website Copywriting | SEO Copywriter | Freelance Copywriting
Custom Copywriting is the number one source for all of your SEO web copywriting needs. ... Are you in search of the right words to promote your product or service? ...www.customcopywriting.com - 17k – Cached

Google:
Website Copywriting | SEO Copywriter | Freelance Copywriting
Custom Copywriting is the number one source for all of your SEO web copywriting needs. We are the fastest growing web copywriter in the nation because we ...

www.customcopywriting.com/ - 18k - Cached - Similar pages

Experiment with your tags and don't stop until they are working well for you. Getting these right is going to make a big long-term impact on your site – and your online profits!

And remember, on keyword phrases, make them very specific. If you currently say "our vacation packages," use "our Bahama island vacation packages" instead. If you are selling "day spa services," use this as your keyword phrase instead of simply "services."

Snippet Content

As we mentioned above, the "snippet" is the text that appears underneath the title on the search engine results page. Some people read snippets, others scan them, and some don't look at them at all. But whoever you are dealing with, this little group of words can get people to click on the link to your web page/site, if it's written well. With Google and Yahoo, they usually just take a small chunk of text from your page and use that as the snippet. Google's is usually shorter than Yahoo's, and Yahoo will many times use the description tag.

So, one way you can influence snippets is by writing solid copy on the page: benefits oriented, keyword rich copy that can convert as well as be great description tag copy. Influencing the snippet copy is one of those things that usually is missed by most people when they are thinking about improving their website.

How else can you influence your snippet? For Yahoo, place your keyword phrases together near the beginning of the descrip-

One last secret: place a benefit statement next to your keyword phrase in the snippet. Example for the keyword phrase "art supplies":

The most extensive **art supplies** online

…Stop searching. All of your painter brushes, oil based paints and other **art supplies** are available in one place. **Free shipping!** www. NelsonBrothersArtSupplies.com/ 35K – Cached

Free Shipping is of course, your benefit statement/call to action. Try this technique out!

tion. For Google, do the same thing, just in the body text, or main copy section of the page. How long are snippets usually? Around 150 characters.

Other Stuff: Alt Text, Text Hidden in Images

You know those big beautiful headings you see on the fashion or department store websites? Did you know that they are almost always invisible to the search engine spiders? It's true and most people don't realize the impact. They may even be using their keyword phrases. But, it's not going to do them any good with the spiders. How can they change this? Tell your designer to code these words as headings – not images. That will solve the problem.

Alt text is descriptive text for images on the page. This is another one of those areas that people forget about. Many images don't have any text to describe them. This can be fixed by simply writing some copy, using a keyword phrase of course, and giving it to your designer to place into the code. You'll know if you have it in place if it's there when you place the cursor over the image.

Something that Isn't Really Talked About

We discussed keyword penetration earlier. We discussed how the 3-8% range is probably about right. However, there are certain sites that only require 1-2% keyword penetration. Take casino, drug and adult sites for example. They are well known for spamming the search engines and essentially "over" optimizing. What does this mean exactly? It means they keyword stuff and create scraper sites and do other things that are generally not a very good idea. Advice: Don't load your site up with tons of keyword phrases. It's never a good idea.

There is no easy and fast way to write and rank! If you are looking for shortcuts, you're not going to find them in the world of SEO.

A Word or Two on Dynamic Content

Dynamic pages are generated by a software program whenever someone requests your page URL. Search engines also call them up. Dynamic pages work by using template and database information. They are usually controlled by the IT Dept, site developer or database people in your company. As such, they usually don't understand that there are SEO copy considerations for these dynamic pages. Basically, you'll need to influence and manage this process to ensure three things that usually go un-done on these types of pages:

- Make sure the pages have title tags
- Make sure that all the titles are different on all the dynamic pages
- Make sure the titles are written using the rules I have outlined in this chapter.

The IT or database person may need to create a new title field to the database, and it's very important that they do this. Working with them closely will usually assure a positive outcome.

That's essentially it with dynamic content!

Does the Content Work? Analyzing the Results

I discuss this in other parts of the book, and although it seems obvious to analyze your results, I wanted to mention it here as well. So, now that you have optimized your content, is it working? This will take time of course, but within two to three months (sometimes much sooner), you should be seeing an impact – if it's working that is! Check your keyword phrases and see if you come up. Be sure to look in multiple search engines, I check Google, Yahoo and MSN monthly. Look at your link popularity. Your links should be steadily increasing.

How about your search traffic? Are you getting more leads/referrals from the web? Check your log files; look at your traffic through your analytics provider (ClickTracks or WebTrends). Finally, how many people who end up on your site are being converted to a sale? That's the most important, of course. If the results aren't what you want, keep trying to improve your site. Look at the suggestions in this chapter again, re-read other important chapters on keyword research and writing content. Talk to others and see what they think.

One way or another, with enough hard work, you'll get the rankings – and the conversions that you want!

CHAPTER REVIEW

- Write for people first, search engines second.

- Search engines use filtering and ranking to determine which sites get to the top.

- Keyword Frequency = the number of times your keyword appears on the page, use three times on an average sized page.

- Keyword Density = % of the total words on the page divided by the number of times the keyword phrase appears, shoot for 3-8% density.

- Keyword Prominence = Where your keywords appear on the page, make sure they are in headers, high on the page and towards the very end.

- Keyword Proximity = How close each of the words in the phrase are to each other, get them as close as you can in the order that people search.

- Keywords can benefit from being bolded, italicized and linked.

- Meta tag copy needs to include your keyword phrases and be unique for every page – this is an important, but overlooked area of SEO copywriting

ALL THE FLAVORS OF SEO COPYWRITING

Part II

CHAPTER 6

WRITING GENERAL SITE COPY –
A BREAKDOWN ON THE
PAGES YOU'LL NEED TO WRITE

The web is truly a democratic place – if you have an idea or topic that you want to share with others, you can get it online and whammo! you're on your way to building a community, or a market for your product or service. Some people put their heart and soul into it, lots of money, get a little lucky and end up Internet millionaires. Others throw a site together in half a day, don't spend a lot and can't pay people to come to their site. Of course, there are people who throw a site together and still make a lot of money. This is usually driven by a *great idea*. There are also those that put everything into it and don't do well. Following the logic here, that's usually because of a bad idea – or poor execution. Whether you are the one that invests a lot of time, money and resources into your site, the one who doesn't or someone in between, there are certain pages that are important to know about from a copy perspective.

Which pages are most important in regards to using keywords? The Home page, Products and Services, Why Choose Us? and FAQ's. These are the pages that you'll want to be sure to optimize for high impact search rankings. Sometimes they will be landing pages too. As some of the most important pages on your site, they also need to appeal to your potential customers from a sales conversion point of view. They need to really "speak" to the customer. More on that later.

For now, let's get into it and discuss the individual pages…

Which Pages are Most Important?

You know what I'm going to recommend as being the most important page of any site, right? Yes, the Home page. The Home page is like the foundation of your house, without it, your house isn't built right, could fall down and faces an uncertain future. With it, your home is stable, secure and strong. Same goes for your site. The Products or Services page would be next in line. If they don't know what you're selling, how are they going to buy? Because getting your customers *to pay* is also very important for your business, an Ordering or Payment page, integrated with a shopping cart is also critical (If you have something to buy on your site).

There are certain copywriting things you'll want to focus on here. A page about the people (or person) behind the business is an underrated and under-utilized web site page. Whether you call it "About Us" or "Our Team" or something else, it should be a part of every business website. Other pages that have specific and important SEO copywriting elements to them would include FAQ's, and Contact Us.

The Home Page

The number one problem I see with new clients' sites is this: they have an absolutely beautiful (or maybe not so beautiful) Home page with nice images, a good look and feel, contact information and only *three sentences of copy*. They ask me, "Why can't I get ranked on the search engines?" My answer is easy – build more content! Make your site **content rich!** Many of these clients have great off-line businesses, selling hundreds of thousands or even millions of dollars of products to customers around the world. They may have just recently put up a website or aren't looking to drive massive sales off the web. Some of them could though, many of them overlook the potential.

One of my clients who comes to mind is a manufacturer of piping equipment. They have been around for over 50 years and are number two or three in their industry. But, having a website was just never that important. They did have a site, but the home page was exactly as I explained it above: they just slapped it together with a few bad sentences. By revising the home page and the rest of the site, they could expand into new online markets.

I think you get the point – the Home page represents a big opportunity.

When we think about the copy that needs to appear on the Home page, what comes to mind? Well first, it should be the most generic or broad in terms of scope. Let's take the example of a toy manufacturer. Instead of talking about your specific toy lines, you would write more about the *benefits* that your toys provide children. You also want to use your most important and broad keyword phrases here as well. This is the page that you want the very highest ranking for on the search engines. In terms of headers and sub headers, you want them to read almost like headlines – make them stand out, create interesting and thought pro-voking headers.

I'm a big fan of creating three copy sections or paragraphs on the page with three headers. Call it my individual style, but it's a pattern I've used for many clients over the years. Basically, it's a paragraph of 100-150 words in block form first, followed by a bulleted list, followed by another 75-125 word block paragraph. The call to action falls at the bottom of the page. This format has been very popular and helped many of my clients Home pages jump from the 20th page to the 1st or 2nd in a period of a few months. It also is great for scan reading and does a good job of balancing the page design with the page copy, another strategy that I always preach.

About Us Page

One thing I routinely see is a non-existant About Us page. People seem to forget that even though the Internet is just words and images and not a real person engaging them (like at a typical brick and mortar retail store), people still like to know that there are people behind the business. They want to know you care, how you got into your business and what drives you. Perhaps have a picture of the management team on the page. From a content perspective, it's not one of the keyword heavy pages, but the words you use are still very important. You'll want to use this page to put a "face" on the business.

You'll want to make the copy familiar and warm, put some emotion behind it and try and connect with your customers. The other thing about this page – it can mean the difference between a customer choosing you over one of your competitors or not. Why? Well, if it comes down to two sites offering the same exact service for the same price, some people will naturally go with a company whose people they know a little bit about. This brings up another good point – a service business, like a law firm, CPA or copywriter needs to *definitely* have a page about themselves. Those are people businesses! Here's an About Us page I wrote for Provada:

Products Page

So, what are you selling? Do your customers know? Even more than *what* you are selling, what are your customers going to get out of it? What are the *benefits* of your specific products? From a copy point of view, there are a few things you'll want to focus on. First, you'll want to do a quick analysis of what you are selling and categorize it somehow so your customers aren't confused. If you are new to this, you'll want to draw a tree diagram and then for each limb coming off the tree, create a separate page around that product or product group. The product page is where you want to use good keyword phrases and specific language so you can answer your customer's questions before they ask. Assume your customers don't know anything at all about your products and you need to teach them about it. Who, what, where, when and how. Give them all the necessary information they need to help them make a buying decision, or at least a decision on narrowing down the competition.

You'll also want to use some good call to action copy on the page, asking them (or recommending to them) to take some action *right now*! Whether it's a "Ready to order?" or "Call us now for more information!" or "Take a look at what our customers have to say!" This is also a page where you want to have really good balance between the images of your products and the copy that explains them. As you have scanned the web over the past few years, have you seen a few sites that only have images on their product pages and no feature/benefit copy to speak of? I bet you have – it's one of the biggest problems with websites today. There's a picture of the product and a "click here to order" command. This just doesn't cut it anymore. If you have a very loyal customer base, then maybe you can get by with a little less, but you really should assume that your customers don't know anything about your products.

Product Features. Not as important as your product's benefits, but still important. Make sure you write copy that focuses on what your product does and looks like. Some technical specs may be good too, but don't go overboard. What many companies do, especially those who know very little about good copywriting, is write *only* about features. Although this is better than having *no* copy, it's still a long way from optimum. Men are more often guilty of this than women. Women have a much more intuitive feel for how the product can and should integrate into someone's life. They usually – not always, make better SEO copywriters, partly because of this fact. And here's the other thing about writing features and benefits: people seem to have a hard time knowing the difference. They confuse them all the time, or simply don't know really how their product impacts their customer's life. Here's where one of the other all-important tenants of copywriting comes into play – *ask them how your product benefits them.* They will tell you. When they do, turn their answer into some great, hard-hitting, conversion friendly product website copy!

Services Page

Most of the same things mentioned above in the Products page will also apply to a Services page. Writing about your company's services does have some important differences. The first thing to consider before you write is whether your service is a commodity or not (Think law services). If it is, you'll want to typically have less specific copy on the page and try to get them to contact you – either by email or phone so you can sell them in a more personal way. If your service is not so commoditized (think a dog walking service), then you'll probably want to be more detailed in your copywriting so people who don't understand what it is will get their questions answered up front.

It also helps to sell them or qualify them a little up front. Of course, you'll also want copy that tells them how to contact you for inquiries, but if they found you, they probably are already pretty well qualified. Also – with a non-commoditized service, it could be relatively new, so you may not have too many competitors. Getting them to contact you for the sale won't be as important.

Local search. It's been all the rage in the past couple of years. For a service like a barber shop or pet groomer, you'll want to definitely use geographically specific keyword phrases like "Springville barber shops" or "Missoula pet grooming" in your Service page copy. The local area, is where most, if not all, your customers will be coming from, so you want to be sure to do this.

Order/Payment Page

What type of copywriting do you think an Order or Payment page should have? Probably a very detailed explanation of how they order or pay; make it clear and specific. Maybe list out the steps to take. You'll also want to include copy that makes them feel like this is a safe and totally secure trans-action. Many sites make this mistake. Think about when you go online and make a purchase. You want to know, beyond a shadow of a doubt, that it's a secure transaction – and that this is a reputable company who won't take your money.

You'll also want to write some content that speaks to your return or exchange policy. Again, answer the question before it is asked. If you don't have a return or exchange policy, maybe think about establishing one.

Most of all make your order/payment page copy very simple and easy to follow.

Here's a great Order From from one of my client's sites:

FAQ's

It has been great to see so many websites decide to write a Frequently Asked Question's page. This is almost *always* a good idea. One of the great benefits to having a website and an online business is the fact that you can automate so many parts of your business and eliminate overall costs. Think about it – if you have a very good, comprehensive FAQ section would you need to spend money on having a Customer Support function? Maybe not. Couple your FAQ page with a robust Forum tool and then you'll really have something! Not sure what questions to feature on this page? Again, ask your customers, they will tell you. Send a short survey to them, or check out the competition. What type of FAQ section do they have?

In terms of the type of copywriting you'll want to use here, make it very specific and keyword rich. When people are surfing online, they usually have a question or two about what they are looking for. They may even put their search words in the form of a question. If you have the copy for that question on your FAQ page in the same exact way (or close), your site will come up first! Nice little bonus there. Lots of my clients don't think about that, but it can make a real difference.

Finally, I would make the question and answer copy short and to the point. Remember, people are scan reading. They want super quick information.

Contact Us

You do have a way for customers to contact you, right? Hope so. If you do, let's talk about the copywriting for that page. The biggest problem I see is that people make this page too content heavy or too content light. Or they make it confusing. All you really need is a one paragraph section on this page. For most sites, all you need are three to four short sentences about your interest in having your customers contact you for any and all needs and then your detailed contact information – email addresses and phone numbers, street address, city, state, zip.

Also a word about phone numbers. Give your customers a way to call you! There are so many sites out there that don't give their customers this opportunity. Also, provide a physical street address. People want to know that there's some level of permanency to your company. A street address provides this credibility.

Places to Expand Content

So, if you know a few things about search engine optimization (SEO) - hopefully you do now that you're a good way through this book - then you know that one of the most important things about keeping up is to add more relevant content to your site. But how do you do that exactly? Which pages are the easy targets for expansion? How can you make it simple? I have some copy recommendations based on tried and true, real life experience. If you have the same site up that you did a year or even two years ago, then you're in dire need of a copywriting update. Of course, it does depend heavily on what type of business you are in, but it's really a good thing for all online businesses to do. So, let's discuss it.

● Products/Services

This is an easy one to expand. Because many sites don't have much copywriting depth in this area to start with, it can be an easy fix. Again, think specific and think product groupings. You could easily turn a one page Products page into ten new pages in three days. Google will take notice of this and hopefully reward you with some higher rankings. If you are a day spa and your current Services page has a quick general blurb about your massage therapy, facials and mud baths, make each of these their own sub-pages under the larger Services page and then write more specifically – both in the language that entices your potential customer and in the keywords that you are using. You could go from ranking well for "spas in Concord, CA" to maintaining your ranking for that phrase and also adding new rankings for "massage therapy in the bay area," "facials in bay area" and "mud bath services in the bay area." And that only equals one thing: NEW CUSTOMERS!

• Articles

We discuss at length the power that articles can have on your business in an upcoming chapter, but just a few extra words of advice here as well. If you want to make your site more robust, more sophisticated and more respected, then writing a series of articles is a no-brainer. Again, you could have instant web site copywriting breadth with a simple series of five articles a month for six months. Just to break a commonly held myth out there too – people do read these! They typically also read them word for word, sometimes print them out, refer back to them over and over and share them with friends. Talk about powerful! If you write them from a point of conviction and passion and knowledge, all the better.

Two other things: Be sure to have a separate section on your site dedicated to articles and give people the chance to use them on their sites or blogs as well.

• Resources

There's not a whole lot of copywriting that goes into a Resources page. Another name for this could be Links of Interest, or Other Sites. The important thing from a copywriting perspective is to mention that you have a Resources page on other pages within the site. It could go towards the bottom of the page, but this will help people find it and use it. The other value of this is in the link building process (big SEO benefit) with other sites in your industry.

• Forum

With this section, your customers write the copy for you! You'll want to review all the postings and threads before they go up, but this is a great place to build out content and usability for your customers. It helps in the *online experience* you want your customers to have. It also does one other very important thing from a copywriting point of view: it keeps your visitors on the site much longer and increases your chances of having them jump to other pages on your site and read the copy on those pages!

● Adding to Short Existing Pages

If you want to add content fast and easily, look to your existing pages. Adding a paragraph or two to your Home page or About Us page is a quick and somewhat painless activity. Why? It's always easier to add to existing content than create it from scratch. One good example of this: our client's projects that require a copy edit instead of all-new copy are usually completed in half the time. So, take a look at your site. Which pages could use a little beefing up? Write those first.

Segment Your Pages As Needed

On many large sites, especially for those that have been around a long time or multi-national corporate sites, there is a need to categorize or group sections. An example of this would be on the "About Us" pages that you come across. Instead of putting all the information – everything under the sun and about the company – on the same page, split it up. Place "Company Profile" on one page, "Latest News" on another, "Board of Directors" on still another and "History" on the last.

You should also do this for other sections on your site that have lots of sub-categories.

Pages that Many Companies Forget About

The first page that people forget to write is a Privacy Policy and/or Terms and Conditions. This is important to write from a legal perspective. It's also good to write one for your customer's peace of mind and your need to build credibility with them. If you don't know the first thing about writing one, take a look at your competitor's web sites. Read theirs. Don't steal it, but use it as a template for what you should do. Be sure to include copy that speaks to the information you will be asking for and collecting, the customer's rights, the fact that the site will be updated on a regular basis and some language about how they can contact you if they have a question about their privacy rights. Terms and Conditions would be more about what they can expect if they buy from you.

Another page that people forget about is the FAQ section. Because many companies don't think in terms of their customer's questions or point of view, they simply forget about writing one. This page should be very easy to write. Your customers previously asked questions can almost write it for you!

"Why are we Better?" This is a great page to have. How are you better than your competition? Some of your customers will want to know. Making it a stand alone page can be very powerful. Companies that *do* use this type of copy usually put it on the Products or Services pages, but if you have a compelling story to tell here, give the topic its own site space. You'll quickly see that customers will go to that page a lot – sometimes more than the About Us page. Make the copy benefit rich!

A Unique Case: The Long "Direct Response" Sales Letter Site – Copywriting Techniques

What are long direct response sales letter type sites? Chances are you've seen them. Many of you may even own a few – there are many out there. These sites are the ones that have the long, scrolling Home page with the testimonials, positive, benefits oriented mega copy, multiple calls to action and no mention of price – until the very end. I have written a few of these and bought from a few too.

There are lots of books written on this topic. The reason for this is these sites are all about making money – for better or worse. Personally, I'm not a big fan of direct response sales letter type sites, but I know there are many out there that are doing well and there are many customers who have purchased products from them who are satisfied.

Because these sites are unique, there are certain ways to write them, and if you want to go with something like that, you'll need to know how to do it well. The key with this kind of SEO copywriting is that you follow a specific formula in crafting the words. Here are the important elements:

1. Communicating with emotional appeals: all people buy based on emotion, but with this kind of copy, it rules the day. Essentially, you want to tap into the hopes, fears, anger, frustration, egos and/or pocketbook of your prospects. Here are some phrases that you may want to use in the copy:

   - Could you use some ideas on how to jump start your online business so you start making huge streams of passive income – even while you're sleeping?
   - Can you imagine a life where all your credit cards are paid off – and you have plenty of money in the bank for your children's college education and your retirement?
   - Don't you hate it when you're rejected by women time after time – do you want to know the secrets that every Casanova knows - that will make the ladies fall at your feet?

2. Allow your satisfied customers to tell their stories, explaining in detail why your product or service worked and how it's impacting their lives every day.

   - This could be in the form of testimonials, case studies and/or proven statistics.
   - When prospects read these, they start thinking to themselves, "This could work for me too."

3. Play on the Psychology of Human Intention/Persuasion – this is the device that wraps it all together

   - Promising something early in the copy and repeating it throughout the communication – gets the prospect to commit.
   - Getting them to actively participate in the communication – making it interactive. This involves having them answer a quick survey or a couple of questions right in the body of the copy.

- Asking a question early in the copy that makes them mentally commit to what you are proposing.
- The "Ginsu Knives" 25 Approach – we all remember this commercial; it was on TV for many years. The power behind their advertising success, as you may recall was showing you what you would get for $29.95, and then throwing in a bunch of other things, like the carrot peeler and the tomato garnisher, etc. and telling you that others would charge you $100 or more for all of these items, but here, for a limited time, you get everything – the knives, the peeler, the garnisher – oh, and a set of corn holders too – not for $29.95, but for only $19.95 – but only if you act NOW! Well, after all that, the $19.95 doesn't sound so bad, right? This is a great psychological copywriting tool that will work very well.
- Getting your prospects to accept suggestions as facts. Example: *What will you do with the extra time you'll have to spend with your family after you purchase this product?* This immediately puts the idea in their heads that they will gain more time – time they can spend any way they choose once they act on your offer. This could be true for some of your past clients and untrue for some of them as well, *but it communicates to your prospect that extra time is a possibility if they act now and buy the product.*
- Placing phrases in the copy that tell them exactly what you want them to do, without it making it seem like you are, i.e. *Don't you want to enjoy the same good looks as others who buy "Revolution Hair" Thickening Gel and regain your youthful appearance?* With this, you are telling them to "buy Revolution Hair Thickening Gel" right smack dab in the middle of the sentence.

4. Use Free Bonus Offers and Guarantees: Two to three free offers promised to them regardless if they buy or not – as well as the standard product guarantee - can be very powerful copywriting

devices. You use these toward the end of the copy. For the bonus offers, make it something that has value and tell them what the dollar value actually is. Here are examples of each:

- Free Bonus Offer # 1: The Top 10 Reasons Why Real Estate Agents Should Use Foreclosure Listings in their Business – Valued at $49
- 100% Money Back Guarantee on Your Order – if you aren't satisfied, simply send us an email to let us know and we'll gladly refund your payment.

5. The Power of Effective Headlines and Sub-Headlines: It seems that we are all programmed at birth to be subconsciously drawn to headlines. They give us something to focus on at first glance, give us a reason to read on and make a promise. They help us through the mental process of making the decision to go forward with the rest of the story – or stop and go on to the next thing, something better that speaks to us. Bottom line – the headline and all the others that follow in this type of SEO copywriting SELL, over and over again. Here are a few good examples:

- Learn to Play Guitar like the Pros in 2 weeks Without Knowing How to Read Music!
- Want to Know the Secret Online Marketing Techniques that Made Me a Millionaire in 1 Year?
- Subliminal NLP Techniques to Get People To Do Anything You Want – Tonight!

6. The Close: Make it short, to the point and urgent. Give them a time deadline if you think that would help. And also – employ your call to action. What works well here? *Stop Putting it Off! Start your Free 1 week Trial Now! Or Get Your Free Reports when you submit your email address below or Click here and You're on Your Way to Instant Online Profits!*

Here is an example of direct response copy I wrote for a new Home page:

"Learn Proven Short Sale Strategies from an Expert Real Estate Attorney TODAY!"
...and make $10K-40K or more per transaction!! Here is the one great way to get involved in short sale foreclosure investing now!

"The very first month that I implemented John's strategies – I was able to close 2 deals... what a difference knowing the basics can make!"

- Jane Doe, Realtor

Dear Real Estate Professional:
Can you believe what's going on in the real estate market? Everything has changed from the high flying days where you could make money without even trying. Foreclosures are happening all over the country and lenders are going out of business. Sounds like a doomsday situation right? Well, quite the contrary – at least for real estate professionals like us.

Hi; my name is John Taylor. I am a licensed real estate attorney and have been practicing for over 10 years at some of the highest-profile law firms and real estate companies in the nation. I am a published legal author and have had a great corporate career. I have been in-house counsel for the largest owner/operator of multi-family housing and **had the privilege of making clients and partners I worked for very wealthy,** while pounding out 80-90 hour work weeks.

I'm not a superstar real estate guru who goes around the country making empty promises – I'm the real deal, the guy in the trenches every day, doing deals, making things happen!

So, Why am I Qualified to Teach Short Sale Investing?

A few of things I've been able to do for my clients:

• Managed a $500 million multiple-asset acquisition for a Billionaire in Los Angeles.

• Developed many high-profile projects including hotels, resorts, retail malls and mixed-use properties.

• Represented some of our nation's largest banking, lending and financial institutions in multi-million dollar real estate deals

• Landlord representation for a Fortune 10 company's headquarter relocation

And here's the big one...............

• **Lender representation in hundreds of foreclosures.**

As you can see from the list above I have personally participated in over 2500+ real estate transactions, and I can say without hesitation that I have made other people extremely wealthy. <u>But what about us?</u>

<u>When you think of smart and savvy real estate tycoons like Donald Trump or other people that have made hundreds of millions, or even **billions** of dollars in real estate, did you assume that they did it on their own? It's not true. Actually...</u>

<u>**I** am the guy that they "leveraged" to manage and run their real estate deals. Essentially, they became the deal "getter" and I became the deal "doer." This has worked well for them, **but what about us?** I don't know about you, but I simply wanted more!!!!</u>

<u>Look, I was once just like you – working hard, hardly spending any time with the ones I loved. There had to be a better way**. Fore-closures** were my answer. I took what I was already doing for my employers, and decided that it was my turn to get rich, and decided right then and there to "TAKE ACTION!"</u>

Now that I have mastered the game of leverage and switched my focus from deal doer to deal getter, I am sharing these secrets with real estate agents everywhere. I can teach you how to find the deals, how to negotiate and close the deals, how to streamline the process and avoid the pitfalls, and **how to make sure you get paid!!!**
And isn't that what it's all about...of course, but you know what? You'll also being HELPING a lot of good people out of a bind. And that makes it feel good too.

So what makes me qualified to teach you?

Well, here is what I am not....I am **not** an agent who got sick of doing my own deals. I am **not** a trainer who is recycling their investor training to make it fit for real estate agents. And I'm for sure **not** a guy with just little more than an idea and a computer. I am a highly trained, highly sought after "doer," **who is making more money that I ever thought possible, simply doing the same things I did for over 10 years for rich people. It really is very simple – it's called maximizing your potential and living your dream!**

If you are a real estate agent who wants more than you're getting, I can help. I will show you systematically how to do short sales correctly and ethically, adding a new revenue stream to your total commission income!

"Your short sale teachings are powerful tools. I know I can turn what I've learned into some big-time cash flow."- John Doe
By the way, if you haven't signed up to receive my e-newsletter filled with dozens of tips, advice and other Short Sale Strategies – I strongly suggest you do so now. Plus - **It's absolutely FREE!**

First Name:
Last Name:
E-Mail Address:

Back to creating your Short Sale Investing success...

Simply put, you need to "TAKE ACTION NOW."

Remember how I mentioned that I really felt the need to get out of corporate America? Perhaps this sounds familiar...While my very wealthy employers got to go to cool parties, drive nice cars, live in nice houses, and take nice vacations with their families, **I dealt with the hard work (80-90 hours per week) of making them money. And it was tough!**

While they were on the beach with their family, **I was missing precious time with mine.** You know, there's nothing worse than having to look your child in the eyes and say, I'm sorry I can't make it this time, maybe next.

Quite frankly, I was tired of breaking my kids' hearts, hearing them choking back the tears as I explained that Daddy needed to do important work on nights and weekends, missing yet another game, event, party, etc. In order for things to change, I realized that I needed to change. **I made a vow to never let my time at work get in the way again.**

I Know What You Must Be Thinking...

"...this guy is an idiot - if I knew everything he knew, I would make millions in real estate, NO PROBLEM." I mean let me get this straight...

- John went to law school for 3 years
- John lead real estate transactions for some of the world's most respected companies

- John became in-house counsel for the largest publicly traded company of multi-family residential real estate
- …and then eventually was retained to run a $500 million dollar acquisition project (yea really fun, I promise), **but wasn't rich? How is that possible????**

Trust me, I get it, I mean it makes sense, and I was saying the same thing to myself all the time. But I gotta tell you -- I just didn't think I could do what the guys that were rich were doing, i.e. <u>FIND THE DEALS!!!!!</u>

Well, finally, I got fed up, and after 10+ years of making other people filthy rich I decided to branch off, and use these same techniques to make money for myself. I needed to find someone to "leverage" to find me the deals. So, I opened a company, headquartered in Torrance, California, and we started working with real estate agents to help them get their deals done.

And you know what? I quickly learned something in the process…

Those who "leveraged" themselves were the ones that got rich, those who didn't **got nothing.** Remember when I said that the millionaire real estate tycoons "leveraged" me to make them money, well now **you can too.**

I PERSONALLY AM INVITING YOU TO A DAY LONG
SEMINAR ON SHORT SALE INVESTING. UNLIKE ALL
THE OTHERS, THIS IS THE ONE THAT WILL FINALLY
TEACH YOU EVERYTHING WITHOUT HAVING TO
FORK OVER $3,000
<u>Sign up NOW</u>

Look, I am a <u>numbers</u> kind of guy. It seems like it's always been that way actually. As a kid, I recall being in love with math. When all the other kids got C's on their tests, I was getting a perfect score. I guess it just naturally translated into a love for studying the market. Let's face it - It's been an incredible rollercoaster ride over the past 15 years. Knowing the stats, understanding historical trends, and knowing what numbers mean makes ALL THE DIFFERENCE!

ATTENTION All Real Estate Agents!

As you may know, the current market is primed for Real Estate agents that want to perform short sales. Informed investors are still getting rich, but it's much more competitive, and the deals are getting more risky for the novice investor. How do I know? **<u>I've studied the numbers!</u>**

Real estate agents are getting more listings than ever before and selling homes quickly because they are able to price them so much below market value (Up to 25% in some cases!).

The real estate agents we are working with are **<u>closing more deals, making more money and smiling all the way to the bank</u>** – **even in this down market!!!!** They "leverage" me by learning how to do these deals right, and they further "leverage" me when they are stuck in the deal, or have questions about the right way to do it.

SO WHAT ARE YOU WAITING FOR, COME TO OUR SEMINAR ON SHORT SALE INVESTING. STOP PUTTING IT OFF –
THE TIME IS NOW!
<u>Sign up today</u>

As I mentioned earlier, the foreclosure market has heated up in the past couple of years. There's a huge difference in what's going on year over year. In fact, I have found myself **training a lot of agents on the laws** - specific to foreclosures, so they go into the deal educated. That's right - there are differences in these deals that you have to be aware of.

And you know what?

You may even find yourself with 2-3 listings at a time, and this can be stressful! How do you manage multiple deals? I'll tell you what I see. Agents that <u>are not working within the law</u>, end up losing the profit they make on their deals because they have to use the $$$ to correct and settle the legal problems they made for themselves!

The good news is that these problems are easy to avoid if you have easy to follow checklists and simple to understand summaries of the laws. Having these **will *save you thousands in legal bills***, if one of these deals turns bad.

We see it all the time with agents. But once they start using my checklists, everything gets cleared up. I train them how to stay on the right side of the law...and I can for you too!

"You owe it to yourself to check out John's seminar, I learned more in one day than I did in 3 months with the other guys."-
- John Doe

ENROLL IN OUR SHORT SALE SEMINAR AND SEE HOW YOU CAN EARN ENOUGH INCOME IN ONE YEAR TO LAST A LIFETIME!!
<u>Sign up NOW</u>

Don't be one of the agents that calls me after the deal is done, after it's too late! Stop worrying that something will go wrong and that you'll get a knock on the door with a court summons.

Do you think the wealthy people lose sleep worrying about going to jail or losing millions of dollars with a single decision? Of course not, they have me doing all their work, and making sure that they don't make these same mistakes. You can learn the same! **From ME.**

"There is simply no better information being presented today regarding Short Sale Investing. I highly recommend you attend. It's worth ten times or more what you invest" -- John Doe

So, what am I Offering?

What I'm offering you my friends is an opportunity to emulate my Short Sale results through the training and strategies that only I can provide. There is no one else out there with my background – a real live real estate attorney who has closed countless deals – doing what I do.

Come to our seminar in October! I will teach you – in depth-all the skills I have discussed here and much more. In addition, you'll get *all the insider secrets* that I have learned over the last 10 years, to make sure that after you get the deals, you are able to get paid!

…And isn't this the most important part? Many real estate agents who do foreclosures or short sales end up working 100's of hours on a short sale property, only in the end to lose their commissions to mistakes, or to banks that won't pay them. **This doesn't have to be you.**

During this Seminar you will find out how to:

- Guarantee you will make a full commission on your short-sale
- Learn to be an **"insider"** at the banks and work with them, instead of against them.
- Learn to **reduce the time of the listing** from 4-5 months to as little as 30 days.
- Work through **example deals (real ones)**, and see how they were saved by having the right "tools" and leveraging the right people in your deals.
- Finding the **right escrow company** for your transactions.

I have to tell you - There is no better time than now to start or learn better ways to do Short Sales. My goal for all the agents and brokers out there? To turn a lackluster 2007 into a very profitable year and make 2008 an all time record!!!!

You'll become a bonafied expert – a total specialist in the Short-Sale Market!

Two valuable bonuses (Valued at $198) that you keep no matter what you decide:

Bonus #1:	***"The Insider Secrets to Short Sale Success."*** *(Value: $129)*

With this great bonus, I'll show you...

- The **difference** between the successful and unsuccessful investor
- How to **talk** to homeowners facing foreclosure
- The **easiest** way to make this business work
... plus much more!

Bonus #2:	***"10 Reasons Every Real Estate Agent Should Start Doing Short Sales!" (Value: $69)***

This special guide will explain it all:
- How you can **manage** your leads and find prospects
- How much **money** you can really make in commissions
- How to **talk** to the banks – know what to say, when!

"John Taylor has the ability and as a conference speaker to inform, educate and entertain. We have only had positive reviews of his presentations!"
- John Miller, Real Estate Agent

	To get in on one of my **Short Sale Seminars** NOW...for the incredible low investment of only $99...
1.	Call toll-free at **1-800-999-9999**
2.	**Print out** a registration form and **mail or fax in.**
3.	**Have us call you** for your registration information.

Remember, this is the best opportunity to get into the foreclosure business in over ten years! The **opportunity is all around you**, and now it's right in front of you.

I want you to see how good it can be – there are things that separate the wanna be real estate agents from those that really do. Let's figure it out together!

Looking forward to working with you!

Your friend,
John Taylor, President

P.S. Please join us for our seminar in October, you have nothing to lose and a lifetime of Short Sale Investing learning to gain!!

So there you have it, everything you need to know about the almighty direct response type sales letter copywriting technique. Remember, it will take a while to construct this kind of copy and it may take a few tries to get it right, but if done right, and with a high quality product or service - can make you a lot of money, very quickly.

CHAPTER REVIEW

- The Home page is your most important copywriting spot on your site, use your keywords and give prospects a reason to click on other pages.

- Having a main Products or Services page is critical, but be sure to also write unique copy for each of your individual products or services and place it on separate pages.

- Copywriting on your FAQ page should be specific and provide thorough answers.

- Places to expand content could include more Product or Service pages, articles, a blog, Resources page and/or a forum.

- Don't forget about your Privacy Policy and Terms and Conditions pages!

CHAPTER 7

WRITING SEO ARTICLES FOR FREE PUBLICITY AND INCREDIBLE LINK BUILDING

When you read an article in a magazine or even online about a topic that you find interesting, you usually think the author is probably an expert in their subject, right? If they aren't an expert, then they at least know a great deal about their topic. I mean, they somehow wrote an article that had to be reviewed before it was published and they probably are competing with others for the privilege to write it, right? Given these assumptions, they probably have a few good things to say and have some high level experience in the subject. Do you think these article writers get contacted by people like you who read their article and want to know more? Better yet – are they ever contacted about doing a new project because of the article? The answer is yes! Many, many times probably. Some of them may have to turn down work or pass it to some one else to do – simply because they get too many requests!

So, how does this relate to you and your business? It means *dollars* – sales on the tote board baby! On the web, it means many more things, because writing an article for the web – with a link to your website – is much different than writing an article for a magazine.

So how does it all work?

Article Projects for my Clients

Over the past three years, I have steadily written more and more articles for clients. Currently, I probably write articles for 25% of my clients. What's a typical article project? Ten to twenty articles written on a variety of topics within my client's subject area. What specifically would be topics in a particular subject area? A year ago, I wrote ten articles for the hot air balloon company we discussed earlier, California Dreamin. They provided sunrise rides in their beautiful big hot air balloons as well as exciting bi-plane rides. They wanted to increase their website's search engine ranking and wanted to try having some articles written to see how it impacted online leads. Here are the articles I wrote for them:

- The Hot Air Ballooning Experience
- Ride in a Biplane!
- Everything you ever wanted to do in Temecula
- Southern California: Top Places to Go
- The Vineyards of Temecula Valley: A Wine Region with Class
- Wine Tasting 101
- How Hot Air Balloons Work: The Magic of Quiet Flight
- Fun Facts about Hot Air Balloons that You Didn't Know

- The Largest Hot Air Balloon Festivals in the World
- Flying a Bi-Plane: The Thrill of the Adventure

Obviously, these were a lot of fun to write! Having been in a hot air balloon before, I knew the total exhilaration that they provide – it is truly something everyone should do at least once in their lives. Not all the companies I write articles for have such an interesting topic to write about! I've written articles about nuts and bolts too. One thing that is true – it's fun to set up the articles for my clients with their keyword phrases intact and distribute them out across the web. You never know what good things can happen!

My Personal Experience with Articles

As I mentioned in the introduction, writing and distributing articles on copywriting topics didn't just change my business – they changed my life! Of course, the timing was great too. Today, there are thousands more people out there writing subject articles on every topic imaginable, but once you write yours, they may continue to make a big impact for a long time. Upon checking recently, one of my articles entitled "Search Engine Optimized (SEO) Copy - The Down and Dirty Details" that I wrote three years ago was listed on 315 sites on a Yahoo search and 205 sites on a Google search. Some of the sites they are found on are giant web powerhouse players too, like Site Pro News **26** and Web Pro News **27**! This means that every day, many people all over the world may read these, see my URL and email me regarding some business they would like done. How would you like some of the same free advertising benefit? IT WORKS!

It's Viral!

I remember checking my articles out online after I had them sent out. I watched as the first fifty sites became the first hundred which became the first two hundred and so on. At the height of their popularity, some of the articles were on over a thousand sites all over the world. Some high traffic, some not so high traffic. But, the point is that your articles could be picked up by thousands of sites, almost overnight. If they are well written, popular and give some great advice, they could get to that number very quickly. Think you'll get some calls for potential business? You bet.

I even know some other copywriters out there who did the same thing and ended up with *tens of thousands of sites* hosting their articles. It **can** be done. I think they eventually brought on a bunch of new writers when they couldn't handle the flow of new business inquiries!

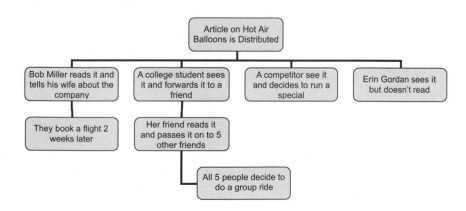

PLR Articles

Private Label Rights (PLR) Articles have been around for a while and are used by some companies out there to beef up their site content. Essentially, they are quickly written subject articles, provided by certain online article writing "factories" that are apparently supposed to be *original*. They are also cheap - many of these PLR Article providers charge less than $10/article.

The problem is that they *aren't* always totally original - which means you'll have to re-write them, they don't always use the keyword phrases that you should be using and worst of all - many of these PLR articles are dry and meaningless - they lack substance and soul. Personally, I would steer clear of this type of content.

What does a Real Article Look like?

Here is an actual article of mine that went out a few years ago:

Ad Copywriting: Building Brand Equity One Word at a Time

Need an article for your Newsletter or Ezine? Feel free to use this one!

You can publish this article in your newsletter or Ezine for FREE; we just ask that you help us out with the following:

1. Don't alter the article in any way; it must remain in its current formatting with the identical copy. Please include the Byline at the end of the article, including a link to our website, Custom Copywriting

2. Please tell us where it's going to be published

3. You agree to indemnify Custom Copywriting and its employees from and against all losses, claims, damages, and liabilities which arise out of its use.

Article Summary: Hard to Read, Difficult to follow web site copy can be magically re-born by sticking to some tested rules.

Ad Copywriting: Building Brand Equity one Word at a Time

By Jon Wuebben I Professional Website Copywriter

Ah...advertisements, those wonderfully adorable little vignettes that come to us at all hours of the day, seven days a week, fifty two weeks a year. Seventy percent of them are ineffective. Probably more than that actually. And a lot of them can become very annoying.

But then there are those ads – those special ads that stand out and make you say, "Hey, that was a really good ad!" For us in the ad and copywriting business, that may happen a little more often, simply because we tend to pay more attention to things that interest us. But, when it happens for you, what do you think it is that is making you take notice?

Well an advertisement is obviously an image, coupled with a message (copy). But not all the time. Sometimes it's just an image, other times it's just copy. But more often than not, it's a combination. Well, in this article, we're dealing with the Copy aspect. And in my opinion, that's the most important part. But then again, I'm a little biased! Well, anyway, here are some tried and true methods for making sure you have written world-class ad copy that can begin to build Brand Equity.

1) Clarify the Goal of the Ad Copy.
What do you want the consumer to do after seeing the ad? Do you want them to buy your product, "call now," go to your website, or send for a brochure? Whatever it is, make sure you know before you even put pen to paper (or hands to keyboard). The "Call to Action" as it is known in its classic form, is without a doubt one of the two most important parts of the ad copy. The other is the...

2) Headline! Headline! Headline! Headline!

We've heard it a million times – a great headline can make a business rich overnight. And it's true. The headline is critical. The mission is to reach out to the consumer as they are paging through that magazine, surfing the web or channel surfing their TV and magically bring them into the ad. How are you going to do it? Do a lot of brainstorming before you decide on the headline. That will help flesh out the idea. When you have the right one, you'll know. It will easily stand above the rest.

3) Write like People Talk.
This is not a research paper! Not even close to it. This is a conversation with your customer, only it's written (or spoken) and it's one-way communication. That is, the potential customer can't ask questions of the ad. Or can they? Well, at least not now they can't, but definitely in the future. Great ad copy is persuasive prose that convinces the consumer to buy. Write like people talk. You'll bond with the potential customer that much more.

4) Be Inventive. How do you make your ad really stand out? How about creating a new metaphor? That's a tough one. But it has been done. Maybe you can find a unique way of expressing an idea or concept in the ad. A new way of approaching an old subject can really bring it to life. This is also one step that most copywriters forget about.

5) Don't use Clichés!
Nothing more really needs to be said on that one. Just make sure they don't creep in.

6) Make Every Word Count.
This is where ad copywriting really becomes an art form. To make every word count means that you have to get rid of the fl uff and keep the meaningful words. You'll fi nd when you do this that the ad

will take on a whole new look and feel. But the real impact is made when it is read. An ad that keeps only the words that count is an ad that will read very well.

7) Use Short, Snappy Sentences.
Save the long drawn out, adjective fi lled ones for those term papers or essays. That's the only place they belong. People are drawn to copythat is punchy, snappy and to the point. Using the present tense and the active voice will go a long way to getting you there. Good ads always use them. You also know it when you see it. And it always makes a better impression.

8) Use AIDA.
Attention-Interest-Desire-Action. If you remember nothing else from this article, remember this. With any advertisement, this is really the "foundation" on which everything else is built. Quite simply, it's: Grab the reader's attention, build their interest, create a desire in them, and make them take action. Of course, it's very easy to say this is what you need to do. The harder question is "how do you do it?" Well think of yourself. What makes you buy something? After you figure that out, then apply it to the copy you are writing.

9) Write about Benefits!
People love to know what's in it for them. In fact, they really want to know what's in it for them! But how many websites or ads have you seen that just talk about how great the product or service is? The goal is to express how this product or service will positively impact your customer's life. The features of the product or the details about the company are important, but they are second string to the first string status of benefits. It takes practice, but it will come. People are just so conditioned to talk about features, that they forget about the most important part...BENEFITS!

That's it! Nine simple steps to keep in mind when writing that next world class, award winning ad! And if you really follow all of them, winning an award could truly be a reality. Because when the right words come together with the right image, that's when people will magically...and faithfully....BUY!

Good Luck!

Jon Wuebben is a professional Website Copywriter, SEO Copywriter and Advertising Copywriter with 10 years experience in B2B & B2C copywriting and marketing. He can be reached at (909) 437-7015, or online at http://www. CustomCopywriting.com for any copywriting project you may have or if you would like more articles or a complimentary Website Copy analysis.

Need a custom newsletter or e-zine article written? Call Jon Today at (909) 437-7015 or email jon@customcopywriting.com for a professional Website Copywriter, SEO Copywriter, or Advertising Copywriter.

Using Keyword Phrases in your Articles

Just like on your site, you'll also want to use your keyword phrases in your articles. How many should you use and how many times each? Probably three to four phrases and then use them three times each in the article. Don't use them any more than this, otherwise it will look like keyword stuffing – and you'll probably get penalized. Also, if you can use the phrases in your headline or subheadline, great. Always a good idea. Once you have a few articles out there, you'll be ranking for your keyword phrases in at least two ways: your site and your articles. The goal? Get all ten spots on the first page! A couple from your site pages, a few from your articles and maybe a couple from some press releases! Be patient, it may take time to get your articles ranked, but if it's a popular topic and enough sites pick it up, you could be all over the web within a couple of months.

In addition, make sure your articles are at least 450 words. Anything less makes it look like the article lacks substance.

How many Articles Do I Write? When and Where do they End Up?

There are many theories on this. Some say write one article a week, some say ten a month, others say get as many out as you can. The key here is to just have a consistent level of output, and distribute them regularly. I would recommend one a week for three months and then see what happens. Take a look at the links you are getting. Go on www.LinkPopularity.com 28 for the full report. After you send your articles out (or have them sent out), they will start showing up within a few days. They will be picked up by article websites like www.findarticles.com, www.goarticles.com, www.articlecity.com, 29 industry specific websites, competitor sites and many others totally unrelated to your business sites. You'll be surprised!

The goal is to make sure they end up on sites in your industry that have a high page rank or have lots of users. This way, you are getting maximum exposure and hopefully, lots of inquiries or new business. I recently checked out where my articles were located and had the following sites show up: www.yourvirtualresource.com, www.businessevolved.com, www.echievements.com 30 and many others. Always interesting to see where they end up!

Adapting Articles You Write for Use on your Site, Blogs, Etc...

The good thing about articles is you can use them for lots of different reasons; you can put them on your site, on a Free Articles page, re-purpose them for blogs, take a whole bunch of them and create an e-book or a traditionally published book, among many other uses. It's all just *information*. How you get that information out to potential customers or users is what's unique. Plus, people have different preferences on how they get their information.

Blogs, of course, are huge, and millions of people go to certain blogs every day.

Others have favorite websites that they often frequent, just because they have been going there for so long (in pre-blog days). Others subscribe to RSS feeds. Some go to article sites, like the ones discussed earlier, expressly to use your article on their site and thank you by giving you a link in return. Why do they want your article? It provides new content for their site. It makes their site CONTENT RICH! And that's what it's all about, right?

It's sort of like this book that you are reading. This is obviously the *print* version. There are, however, other versions, including an e-book, audio book, paper back, foreign language versions and a few others. Your articles function in the same way – use them as many times and in as many ways as possible! Get that *viral* power working for you as soon as possible!

The All Important Personal Section of Your Article

Did you notice the paragraph after my article in the section above? This is where you put your "sales pitch." Basically, you give a short little bio of yourself, how you can be reached and very important: your URL and your keyword phrases. My keyword phrases for this article were: "Website Copywriter," "SEO Copywriter" and "Advertising Copywriter." Those were the words I wanted to rank well for. And you know what? I did fairly well doing that. The personal section is the piece that others are required to use if they also want to use your article on their site. This is how you get the backlink. Be sure that if someone is using your article that they include this all-important section. 98% of people will, but there's always those few who try to cheat you – or worse, they rip you off and plagiarize your content. Your writing is personal, if you wrote it; it should be yours, at all times.

Here is my personal section again:

Jon Wuebben is a professional Website Copywriter, SEO Copywriter and Advertising Copywriter with 10 years experience in B2B & B2C copywriting and marketing. He can be reached at (909) 437-7015, or online at http://www.CustomCopywriting.com for any copywriting project you may have or if you would like more articles or a complimentary Website Copy analysis.

Need a custom newsletter or e-zine article written? Call Jon Today at (909) 437-7015 or email jon@customcopywriting.com for a

professional Website Copywriter, SEO Copywriter, or Advertising Copywriter.

Make sure you also include a Call to Action too, as I did above: *"for any copywriting project you may have or if you would like more articles or a complimentary Website Copy analysis."*

Be Careful – It Needs to Be Something People Would Want to Read

I am always finding articles on the web that are a complete waste of my time! Perhaps you have seen the same thing. You have a topic you want to know more about, say price guides for old baseball cards (which was a real search of mine a few months ago), and you jump on to Google to see what you can find. I saw four or five articles that were only 300 words, filled with keywords and provided absolutely NO real information! How were these articles even submitted in the first place? These so called "articles" are a complete waste of time – both for the person submitting them, because no one will want to link to it – and for the reader, because no valuable information will be acquired.

We all know why these people do it – they want to get a link without doing any work. Well, it doesn't work that way. There really is no easy way to get high quality links. All the short cuts have been eliminated a long time ago. In today's world of search marketing, you need to be savvy – and play by the rules. Hard work, both with online advertising and seo copy-writing will absolutely pay off.

I recently heard Jill Whalen of High Rankings 31 talk about this very subject at Search Engine Strategies in San Jose.

She said that it has become a real problem and pointed out a few examples. I totally agree – if you are going to go to the trouble of publishing an informative article that others will benefit from, you need to make it good. It has to be something people will want to read! If the article comes out poorly solely based on the fact that you aren't the best writer in the world, well then, that's a different issue. All you need to do there is hire a competent copywriter who can write about your topic.

The bottom line? Give your prospective readers more than they expected – and cover a unique angle while you're at it. If your topic has been covered to death, its time to find a different one to write about.

Article Marketer.com [32]

So after you have your article written, what happens next? How do you get it out there and distributed to all the best sites in your industry? How do you get it on those article sites so people can go in there and use your article in their ezine, on their site or in their blog? Well, it used to be that you would have to manually submit them to every single site you wanted it to appear on. This was a very tedious process. Then there were the article sites that promised to distribute your articles to thousands of sites for $19.99. Already sounds like a scam, huh? Well, it was.

As I've mentioned in other areas of the book, I happened upon Maria Marsala and her fantastic business consulting site a few years ago and discovered her article submission service. This was an amazing discovery – she was a big part of why my copywriting business took off the way it did. For $100, she submitted five of my articles to a ton of great places. Probably the best $100 I ever spent.

Maria doesn't offer the article distribution service anymore, but there's a resource out there that is just as good, and I found out about it through her when she decided to move on to other online activities.

It's called Article Marketer.com. This is an exceptional place to go to when you have articles that need to be sent out to the masses. They have taken the art and science of online article distribution and perfected it in every way. For the low fee of $240, you can have an all-access pass to distribute articles through their site for two years! That's a great deal.

I use it for my articles as well as distribution for client's articles and it's very easy to use. Once you have an account, you simply click on the "submit an article" icon and start the process. They ask for an article title, a description of the article, the article itself and the keywords you want to be found under. They also provide a place for your Author box and ask what industry it falls under and if there is a sub-category that would be appropriate.

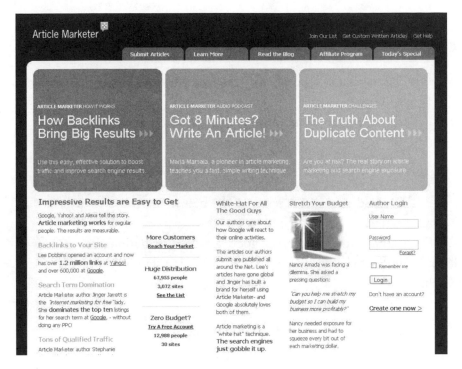

I actually used the site today for a client that specializes in hard drive data recovery and their main industry category was "computers," with a sub-categorization of "data recovery." This article will probably find its way onto hundreds of great sites in this industry and every single one of them will have a link back to his site.

All of it is very intuitive. It's simply copying and pasting and making sure you have everything in the right place. They will review your submission to make sure all the rules have been followed and check to see that it's ready for distribution. Many times, there will be parts of the article that will need to be fixed, such as a grammar mistake or too many keyword phrases used, but all you have to do is fix them and resubmit. This process can take a few days, but is worth it. You don't want an article going out that has problems. Even if you think the copy is absolutely perfect and error-free, trust me, it probably won't be. There have only been a couple of times where I submitted the first time and it went through without an issue.

Simply put, if you want to jump start your online presence in one day, make the decision to follow this schedule:

- 8am-noon: Write four articles on subjects important to your clients
- 1pm: Set up an account on Article Marketer
- 1:15 – 3pm: Submit your articles
- 3:15: Celebrate your accomplishment!

This could go down as seven of the best hours you ever dedicated to your business!

Of course, there are other good article distribution sites out there, but I think Article Marketer is the best. Give it a shot. You won't be disappointed.

Substance in the Body, Site Promotion in the Author Box

Make sure you don't make the mistake that many others do by self promoting in the main body of the article. Remember, this is supposed to be for the benefit of the reader. The fact that you get a nice little back link is just an added bonus. Actually, if you are using Article Marketer, they won't let you submit an article that is heavy on the self promotion thing. Through their review process, which I touched on above, they will catch this every time. But the main reason you don't want to do it is because no one wants to read an article that constantly screams "log on to our site" or "we do this better than everyone else out there." Not good.

You **can** promote the heck out of your business in the Author Box! This is the place to do it. Be sure to mention who you are, what you do, throw in a few good keyword phrases and provide a way to contact you.

Make Sure Your Grammar is Correct

This pretty much goes without saying, but you'd be surprised how many articles out there have major grammar problems – both spelling and format. Some people may think this isn't super important, but with so many exceptional articles out there, it makes your article with misspellings stand out big time. Just be sure to do a spell check and then read it through a couple of times. Of course, it helps to have someone else read it too for another set of eyes. Remember, spell check doesn't catch everything. Plus, it just makes your company look bad. Not too professional.

Don't confuse what I'm trying to say here however. As you can see, I tend to write like I'm talking. Pretty conversational. Ending sentences with prepositions and using fragments (like I did above!) is totally alright. It's part of what makes the copy interesting to read. Just be sure it reads right, and you'll be all set.

Special Characters

You'll need to avoid using special characters like "curly" quotes and em-dashes. They don't translate too well to the web. All you'll need to do to avoid them is copy and paste your article from Word into NotePad. This will take care of the issue. If you are unaware of what I'm referring to, you probably have seen them. They usually appear as question marks or strange number codes on articles you may have seen. Better to get these removed before they get distributed across the web.

Using an Abstract

Something I have seen some people do, especially for white papers, but sometimes for articles too, is the use of an "abstract." This is basically a small section that comes before the article and explains what the white paper or article is about, sort of an Executive Summary. This can be good to have because it basically gives your reader a snippet of what to expect if they read on. It can be another place for keyword phrases, can be placed "above the fold" on the page and is a good way to get the reader to fill out a simple form if they want to go on and read more; a good way to get their email address if you want to use the article as a way to build your double opt-in email list.

CHAPTER REVIEW

- Writing articles shows you are an authority on the subject and gives you high quality links.

- Give your readers high quality; value added information in 450 - 800 words.

- Use relevant keyword phrases in your articles.

- Distribute your articles consistently over time, i.e. never submit twenty on the same day!

- Adapt your articles for use on your blog, site, newsletters, etc.

- Include a keyword rich personal section at the end of your articles so people can contact you!

- ArticleMarketer.com is a great way to send your articles out.

Chapter 8

SEO COPYWRITING FOR PRESS RELEASES

Press releases are one of the "hold over" marketing tactics of the pre-Internet days that have gotten a new lease on life in the world of the web. A standard tool in the public relations arsenal, they have been around for decades. You can't say that for email, blogs, pay per click ads and some of the other new online communication tools. What's interesting is that PR professionals weren't the first to see their new potential in the digital age – SEO guys were.

With Universal Search in full force (see Chapter 17), your Press Releases can show up in the general SERP's too (Search Engine Result Pages).

As with articles, you'll need to use your keywords in press releases too. Unlike articles, distribution can be fairly expensive; at least it has been in the past year or so. When I first started doing them along with all the SEO pros in 2003-2004, they were $40 a pop. Not so now, but still worth the investment. So, what are SEO press releases all about and how do you write them?

Your Game Plan – Put Together an SEO PR Strategy

If you have been writing press releases for a while, you may not need to read everything in this chapter. Writing them is half the battle. You may already know that press releases have incredible value and can be a great way to get some instant exposure. PR's have always had a sort of *panache*, and are usually taken pretty seriously. But let's assume you don't know much about press releases. What should your strategy be around them? How do you start?

Well, the first thing to ask yourself is this: do you have a newsworthy event to talk about? There are lots of things that can fall into this category; a new business announcement, a partnership, a new suite of products, a new service offering, winning an award, hiring a new executive. These are all great things to communicate. A good idea is to put yourself in someone else's shoes and ask yourself whether they would want to read about this topic. If you can't come up with anything, go out and get it! Apply for that award, hire some people, develop a new product. Put yourself in a place where you can write about the good news.

What should your strategy be? Look at your business plan for the year and set up a calendar for your press releases. I would plan to write one every month for a year. See how that goes. If you can't come up with twelve newsworthy items, then maybe you need to start making some things happen in your business! If you're doing a lot of things right, you'll have twenty or more newsworthy topics for the year and your challenge will be going with the *best* ones.

Writing a Release

Copywriting for a search engine optimized press release is different than any other type of online copy. That's one reason why it has a chapter unto itself in this book! As I mentioned earlier, there are certain traditions that press release writing holds and specific ways to write them that are very standard. The great thing about this is that it's like a formula. Once you write one, you can write a hundred. If you've never written one before, the first one will take some time – and maybe a few revisions.

The first thing of course is the *headline*. As you would think, this is very important. It's what pulls your reader in. It should have a little flash to it, maybe an eye-grabbing statistic or benefit. It should be less than 80 characters if possible (You could go as many as 170 if needed). A good one would be *"Beckingham Manufacturing Announces New Service Offering that Cuts Client Hiring Costs by 40%."* That would grab some attention.

Next is the Summary Paragraph. This is a small blurb, usually one to four sentences, right after the headline that says a little bit more about what the PR will cover. (see the sample press release coming up in a few pages)

Here are the rest of the details in order:

1.   The lead sentence: use this key spot to tell the most important information in 30 words or less.

2.   Use the first couple of paragraphs to tell the "who, what, when and where." Use the paragraph after these to discuss the *how* and the *why*. Be sure to focus on making the release interesting to the reader.

3.   Press Releases should be 350 – 800 words, with most falling in the 500-600 range. Make it brief and to the point. Think "lots of facts."

4.   Next, come up with two to three good quotes from executives, customers or other important people and use them in the PR, spaced out so they fall in the 3rd paragraph and 5th, for example.

5.   After the first couple of paragraphs, you may want to have two other paragraphs that basically expand on the topic a bit.

6.   Here is an important one: ***the tone should be objective and neutral. This isn't a place to advertise or get too creative.*** Remember, there is a standard process that all PR's use.

7.   No use of pronouns like "you," "we" or "I."

8.   Use the end of the PR to summarize what you just told them. It could be as short as a sentence, but it will wrap up the story well and give the reader something to remember.

9.   Use two to three important keyword phrases two to three times, separated out in the release - important ones in the headline and first paragraph(Be sure to do some keyword research for this).

Finally, you'll want to include a brief company profile and the company contact for questions regarding the release.

Other Tips and Suggestions

- The first tip would be to try to piggyback off something that's already going on in the news. If a hurricane just struck a major part of the U.S. and you happen to sell boats, this may be a good opportunity to promote something. Pay attention to the news to see what's going on out there and capitalize on it.
- If you are going to use a quote, statistic or other fact that needs validation, be sure to get approval or permission. I have personally seen this happen and it caused a major problem for the company. What happened was a lower level executive was quoted instead of the president of the company. A little ego clash on that one!
- Be honest. This isn't the time to stretch the truth. If you do, you may have just told a lie to 100,000 people. If they catch one, that can't be good for your business. Credibility and integrity are way too important to risk.
- No "passive" voice...make it active instead. Active voice brings people in and emphasizes the subject. People don't feel as close to a passive communication. What does this mean? Example:
  Passive: The house was purchased last month.
  Active: Mark purchased the house last month.
  Passive: The boxes were being stored in the attic by the movers.
  Active: The movers stored the boxes in the attic.
- No need for verbose, flowery or unnecessary adjectives. Keep it simple and concise. Also – don't ever use exclamation marks.

Make Sure the Copy Is Perfect – Avoid These Common Mistakes

What type of mistakes? Grammar would be first. It's gotta be perfect. Also, don't use the word "gotta." Beware of strange characters that may pop up in the release after it's distributed. Copying and pasting can sometimes cause a problem. Another problem that companies encounter deals with email addresses. Instead of using john@accme.com, use pr@accme.com. Using upper case in releases would be the next problem – don't ever do it. Not only is it hard to read, but it just looks bad – and it won't be accepted by the PR sites.

A Sample Press Release:

New Copy Writing Firm Announces Launch

This release is to announce the launch of Custom Copywriting, a new marketing communications firm based in Southern California. The firm serves the copy and marketing needs of small to medium sized businesses nationwide.

Claremont, CA (PRWEB) January 4, 2004 -- Custom Copywriting, a marketing communications company which serves the needs of small to medium sized businesses nationwide has announced their launch.

Custom Copywriting provides website, ad, brochure, direct mail and other copy services to increase the sales and marketing effectiveness of its clients. In addition, marketing consulting and seminar speaking services on marketing and copywriting are also offered.

Over the last five years, their team of writers have provided copy for many Fortune 500 companies, various web firms and non-profits, and other companies. Due to an increased demand for copywriters, they decided to form Custom Copywriting in order to serve the needs of both regional and national businesses.

"We wanted to fill a much-needed niche in the marketing community by servicing small to medium sized businesses who clearly wanted professional, highly effective marketing collateral without having to pay the high fees of an advertising agency. Not all companies can afford to pay a monthly retainer to an agency," said Jon Wuebben, Founder and Managing Director.

For more information, call (760) 451-8700 or contact online at info@CustomCopywriting.com

What Can Happen if You Do It Right

If you are able to put together a killer release that has great buzz and newsworthy flair, you could have a linking juggernaut on your hands. I've heard of a single release bringing in hundreds of new clients for certain businesses. In addition, news organizations may read your release and decide to use your release in a larger feature story. I once had an online business radio show call me to see if I wanted to be interviewed on the subject of SEO copywriting after they read one of my releases.

The other cool thing is this: a release that you write and submit today could still be bringing in traffic two, three or five years from now! Now that's some phenomenal *free* advertising.

The Major Players – Online Wire Services/Press Release Sites

Who are the major players in the PR World? PR Newswire, PRWeb, Business Wire, Marketwire and PrimeNewswire[33] in the U.S. There are others in the international space. On an average day, over 2,000 press releases are sent out by these organizations. Personally, I have used PRWeb and PR Newswire. They are both fantastic and I have nothing but good things to say about them. These are all top notch resources.

Some of them even have a syndicated news feed which essentially makes your headlines available to other sites through XML/RSS. In addition, they will regularly send out email listings of press releases to thousands of media people, bloggers, writers and others who have asked for certain PR's in the industries they cover. Both of these features can dramatically increase exposure for your press release, placing more eyes on your newsworthy story and more mouse clicks on your URL!

To find out more about these PR organizations and to see which one(s) you may want to use, log on to their sites. You may want to use one, or a couple, depending on your preference.

Don't forget about some of the smaller ones[34] too:

www.press-world.com

www.24-7pressrelease.com

www.free-press-release.com

Social Media News Releases

Taking it one step farther would be the "social media" news release, which includes downloadable audio and video files, pdf files, etc. It also gives people the ability to bookmark it in social bookmarking indexes and integrate Technorati tags and links to del.icio.us. To start using a social media release, you'll want to add a multimedia section near the top. Definitely look into doing this with existing or future press releases!

Pitching Your Release to Writers in Your Industry

Many search marketing companies provide an added service for PR distribution by sending them to key writers in your particular industry. This can give your release added fire power because they will put their name behind it and get it to other important people who may blog about it, contact you for more information or just find creative ways to increase overall exposure. Writers are always looking for good things to write about. Their goal is to come up with a good angle that they can use to create an entire series of news stories. The more interest they can generate, the higher their star shines. Plus, it's super competitive out there in the news business. There are lots of reporters looking to out-report others. If you can feed this need, then it means more exposure – and more subsequent sales for your company.

Track the Page Views and Pickups

Be sure to keep track of how your PR is doing out there. Search for your headline on Google and Yahoo. See where it's being picked up. View your stats on the press release site that you used and follow it closely. You'll probably see the most action right after the PR is sent out. Whatever ends up happening, there are always surprises, mostly good ones. What do they say about publicity? There's no such thing as bad news? There's a lot of truth to that.

So, how many people end up seeing your release once it's sent out? Well, it changes all the time, but if you are B2B (Business to Business), you could get 10,000-40,000 page views in the first month. If your company focuses on B2C (Business to Consumer), it's more like 70,000 – 90,000!

The News Organizations are Optimizing Their Websites

Although late to the game, the news companies themselves are optimizing their websites, which means your release may show up high on their site – and high in the search engine rankings too. What's driving this is the whole Universal search dynamic that happened in 2007 (more on this later). News bits – video and text, podcasts, blogs, etc. are now being included in the search results. This is great for your press release, which could be turned into a video news story on the news organization's website.

In addition, there are lots of news search engines that are hungry for good press releases. Some of the major players are Google News, Yahoo News, AlltheWeb News, Feedster and MSN News.

Word to the wise - you definitely want your releases going to Google News and Yahoo News! It's imperative!

It's Getting Crowded Out There

The last thing to consider is that there are more and more releases being distributed every day. Standing out isn't as easy as it used to be. Plus, more press release writers are utilizing keywords in the body of the copy. A few years ago, I observed that only 15-20% of PR's were optimized. Now, it's probably 60-70%. If you want to get noticed, you need to have some very newsworthy releases which are written very well and sent out regularly. If you do this, you'll at least stand out from your competitors, and that may be all you need to do to make PR's really pay off for your overall online marketing efforts and business.

Good luck!

CHAPTER REVIEW

- Using press release copywriting is an excellent way to publicize a new product or event. Use it as a way to integrate other online tactics.

- There's a certain format to follow with press releases – you can't be as creative as you can with articles and site copy.

- Press release copy is a combination of two things: facts and quotes from a company spokesperson.

- Use your keywords!

- The major players in online PR distribution are PR Newswire, PRWeb, Business Wire, Marketwire and Prime Newswire.

CHAPTER 9

GO VIRAL: BLOG/RSS/WIKI COPYWRITING

Is there anything trendier over the past few years than Blogs? Probably not. In 300 years, when the future people of the world look back at the years 2000-2008, what will they say about us? They will say lots of things, but one future observation that is definite: "That generation was blog crazy!" Acknowledging the fact that there is lots of attention placed on this still new and exciting out growth of the Internet itself, there are a number of very positive elements to blog writing that can enhance your goal of being *content rich* on the web.

Of course, blogs are *not* for everyone – or every company. There are still hundreds of thousands of corporations out there that do not have or will never have a blog. Why? A blog is about community – shared information; and for some companies, products or personalities, there would not be an audience – or at least a large enough one. Some also may not want to share this type of information.

But for those that do, consider this: companies used to pay lots of money to interact with and get the attention of a wide group of customers. With a successful blog, they no longer have to pay for that. The prospective or current customer comes to them. With that, let's get into the splendor that is the almighty blog.

A Window Into Your (Somewhat Unfiltered) Thoughts

So what is a weblog or "blog"? Well, 98% of you probably know. But for the 2%, here goes… *a blog is an interactive way of communicating directly with customers or those interested in your products/services by means of writing that is journalistic, informal, opinionated, sensation-alistic and/or unfiltered.* In essence, it's an online diary of your thoughts as it pertains to your website, company or online community. How do you write like this? Well, that's a great question. For those non-writers out there, this is something that you may want to leave to those who can. Casual and informal writing, although it can seem easy – can actually be the hardest to write. Why? This is a dialogue you're going to be having – the people reading your blog can and will comment on what you have to say. Knowing how to write without being defensive or creating a firestorm of back and forth blog battles can be very tricky.

As a window into your somewhat unfiltered thoughts, there is a huge benefit and just as huge a liability. First, the benefit: people like reading diaries, right? Why? Because they reveal "secret" words that were initially intended for the self – or for a few select people. A blog takes that concept and turns it on its head – *they reveal "secret" words intended for the masses* (The Diary of Anne Frank comes to mind, although its mass consumption was an accidental event). The liability then would be the responsibility of keeping the blog current, responding to user feedback and reacting to not so positive posts.

Writing Your Way to Product or Service "Buzz"

So, knowing all of this, what's the biggest advantage to writing a blog and updating it regularly? It could be a one way ticket to fantastic, free PR or "buzz" in the marketplace. You could get a ton of exposure from just one blog posting, because people will pass it on to others or see it through an RSS feed. I'm talking about the viral component to blogs and I'll get into that later in the chapter, but it should be mentioned here as well. Before blogs, there was no way that you could write your way to such quick consumer or end user buzz. That's a testament to the magic of online words and the *"writing your way to wealth on the web"* that this book is all about.

Blogs have made a lot of people and a lot of companies directly or indirectly very wealthy. They've also helped contribute to a more "community based" business environment. In other words, the wall between seller and buyer or company and customer – has been knocked down. Not all the way of course, since every company has things they aren't going to write about to their customers. But, the dynamic is definitely different. Why is this good for you? Again, it's being led by the consumer, and that's what you want. The customer wants to be closer to the company. They want to make sure they are getting exactly what they need and more. Plus, they want to feel less like they are being *sold to* and more like you are *adding value to their precious lives.*

What Do You Write About?

The good thing about writing your blog is that you can write about almost anything under the sun. Do you have a new product and want to get unbiased user reactions? Write about it. Have an opinion about a competitive service? Write about it. Have something you want to get off your chest? Write about it. There really aren't any hard and fast rules about *what* you can blog about. The important thing is similar to being a guest on a talk show: you need to be interesting, or at least *not boring*. Think *thought provoking*. You want to get a reaction out of someone or out of groups of people.

So, how would you do it in conversation? If you are an extrovert or more outgoing person and have a tough time writing this way, think of it in these terms: *how would you say it?* That's a really good way of getting the ideas to flow. If you are feeling a little writer's block is this: just write *something*. It will at least get the ball rolling. That can be half the battle. The people that read your blog can also help with this: they can tell you what to write just by their responses. They can, in effect, lead the conversation and you can simply react to it. Although there are obvious disadvantages to this, it could make crafting your blog, day in, day out, a lot easier.

How do You Start Your Blog?

There are lots of resources out there that can help you get started with a blog setup. We won't get into it here, since this is all about

writing your blog, but some of the most used online places[35] for help in beginning your blog are the following:

- www.blogger.com
- www.typepad.com
- www.wordpress.org
- www.bloglines.com
- www.livejournal.com
- www.technorati.com

Just a note: some people have even abandoned their websites for a blog. Although this may be a good idea for some businesses, I would recommend that a blog be a compliment to your existing website, not something that supplants it.

Although it may sound sacrilegious in the world of the web, some people--gasp--actually don't enjoy blogging or using blogs to get information.

Tagging and Keywords

Like your website, keywords are really important for your blog. However with blogs, there is another important search engine

categorization dynamic called "tagging." Flickr.com[36], the photo sharing website, was one of the first places where tagging was used. Basically, whatever words that best define what your blog posting is about would then become the tags. If you are blogging about online lead generation, then "lead generation" would become your tag. Technorati.com, the blog search engine, uses these tags to find search results, or blogs that are tagged with the same words.

If you are a florist and have a well read blog that covers everything *related to flowers* including roses, your prospective customer can search on Technorati for "rose arrangements" and your blog will come up. See the marketing potential here? People that read your tagged blog can also pass it along to others, and all of a sudden, your words, your search engine optimized blog words, could be in front of thousands of people. Some of these people will be customers.

How do keywords come into play with a blog? Very similar to a website – search engines look for them high up on your blog page, so you'll want to use them in your blog entry title as well as in the entry itself. You don't need to use them as much as you do on your website, but if your blog is about Micro-Brew Beers of the World, make sure you have "Micro Brew Beers" in your title.

In terms of best practices, place the blog name at the end of the title, not at the beginning. In addition, your tag name needs to be found in the title on a tag page.

Also, you'll want to put links like these at the bottom of your post:

Add to del.icio.us | Digg this [37] **| Email this post | Subscribe to this Feed**

Having these in place will encourage the viral aspect of your blog copy.

Use Responses to Your Blog for New Content Ideas

Can't figure out what to write for your articles, press releases or general website copy? Use your blog for new ideas on what you should write about. If you have a blog, you know things have come up that you never thought would have. New topics, interesting comments, radical ideas – they all can be mined for your other online written pieces. Although I don't see many people doing this, it could have a hugely synergistic effect.

Usually, what you see are people getting "blog tunnel vision," whereby everything they write is solely found on their blog – and nowhere else. Even though they wouldn't make it public – a lot of people don't get their information from blogs. They find it on you tube, on your site, through a directory. If you are spending more than 75% of your writing time only on your blog, I would recommend you diversify a bit so you have new content in all the various online communication channels.

Don't Be a "Me Too" Blog

One of the dangers of the blogosphere, as it's called, is related to the sheer number of blogs out there.

Technorati's State of the Blogosphere Report in April, 2007 reported that 1.4 blogs are created every second.[38] That's a ton of blogs! The question: are you blogging just to blog, or do you have a real desire to connect with your user audience in this manner? It sort of goes back to the chapter on SEO articles. I mentioned in that chapter that many people out there are writing things that they call articles, but in reality, they are short, uninteresting copies of other articles out there.

Don't do this with a blog! First, you won't be successful. Blogs are a two way street – they require communication going back and forth between your company and outsiders. Second, you won't get many sales that can be tied to your blog. It may actually hurt you. What if you happen to write something in haste or anger and post it without thinking twice? That could be really bad. It has happened a lot. Of course, it could be good too, in the way that it could simply generate lots of attention, but it's something you have to be really careful with.

I've seen enough blogs to know that there are lots of "me too" blogs out there and they just aren't very good. If you commit to writing blog copy that can benefit your business, make sure it's high quality.

How Do you Write Your Blog's Content From Day to Day?

Blogs can be really good for developing a ritual of constant new content creation. But starting this and really getting into a regular habit can be tough. The good thing is that if you are running your own business, you are already living and breathing your product or service. Blogging about it would just be a natural extension of this. What advice could I give on writing your blog from day to day?

First I would say to make it *different*. Don't always blog about the same subjects, change it up. Throw your audience a curve ball. Next, I would say be provocative once in a while. Put yourself out there and test the waters of reaction.

This can be a little slippery, but with a blog, also very successful. As I mentioned earlier, you could spend a lot of your time just responding to others posts that emanated from your original post.

I would think one of your blog goals should be to grow your user base. The more people that read your blog, the more online influence you can have and eventually – the more sales you can acquire. Remember, if you can get a lot of people reading your blog, you can also sell advertising space! How's that for a new revenue stream? You could spawn a business from your business, and that's what business is all about!

Remember, it's About Community

Blogs are a democracy. Some may argue that point, but I think they are. In this spirit, they are also a community.

Blogs Tap Into the Magical 3rd Party Validation Dynamic

Blogs are really great for another big reason: consumers end up buying from your company not because of *you* so much, *but because of what other consumers are saying about your product or service, in the blog.* I don't know about you, but I always like to know what good old average customers think about something I'm considering buying. Don't get me wrong – consumers can be flat out wrong about something, or spout off an uneducated opinion, but if you read reviews from enough people – you can acquire some great information about a potential purchase. In the pre-Internet days, we relied on magazines like "Consumer Reports", television news reviews and talking to your friends, co-workers and neighbors to get the "buzz." Public relations agencies would get magazines to review products or get it talked about on the morning talk shows, etc.

In the world of blogs, accessing this dynamic for your business could be as close to you as your computer.

Social Media Optimization (SMO): SMO focuses on making changes to optimize a site so its more easily linked to, more highly visible in social media searches on custom search engines like Technorati, and more frequently included in relevant posts on blogs, podcasts and vlogs.

SEO Copywriting and Social Media Optimization

Like its cousin, search engine optimization, *social media optimization* is an important process in the Web 2.0 World. It can help you make the most of your blog copy and everything else you do on the web for your business from a social networking perspective. Basically, it's ensuring that your site is easily connected to those important community type sites, like MySpace, Facebook and the rest.

Whatever you can do to get your site and more specifically, your *blog* copy, included on other blogs, podcasts, vlogs, and also visible on digg. com, del.icio.us and Technorati, the better.

One thing to do is make it easy for visitors to link, tag and bookmark your pages. How can you do it the best way from a copy perspective? Always have fresh, new content on your site, share your content with others and…start a blog.

A Couple Other Important Things that Can Affect Your Blog Copy – and Blog Success

Utilize www.WordPress.org - it can allow you to take advantage of what's called a "post slug," which takes a dynamically named post URL and inserts a high quality keyword in the title.

Also - make sure your blogging software can "ping" the search engines when you add new blog content. You most definitely want Google and Yahoo to spider your blog content!

What is RSS and How Can You Use It To Your Advantage?

When you distribute your content and make it available for others, there is a big mutual benefit. With RSS, you can do exactly that.

RSS is a file format that allows you to "syndicate" content on your blog or website to others. In other words, you can get your content – your "rich" content, on to any other site that would like to have it. Syndication makes your content available to a mass audience, usually for free. You may have seen the RSS symbol on websites you've been on recently. This is usually notated by the words "RSS Newsfeed." This is also a great way to build links back to your site.

Wiki SEO Copywriting

Anyone that has searched for anything in the past couple of years has run into Wikipedia[39]. It changed the Internet forever with its massive Encyclopedia that "anyone can edit." Of course, it's not just a "free for all" where bunches of unregulated or unchecked information is written about; all information must be verifiable and come from a neutral point of view. It's also not a place to post new, original, unpublished research. Like a real hard copy version of an encyclopedia, it's supposed to be made up of facts, statistics, knowledge - things that we already hold to be true and accepted.

So how can you take advantage of this for your business from an SEO copywriting perspective?

Wikipedia allows registered users the chance to create personal pages – on which you can have links to personal and/or business web sites. Many businesses have done just that, and have, in essence, generated another online source for content and links. That's smart writing!

Also, you can install your own wiki using mediawiki.org or wikidot. com.

So you thought all of this online content you were writing was going to be for the benefit of a few hundred people huh?! Try thousands or *hundreds* of thousands. Some super successful blogs even have millions of readers. When you can start making money on your blog solely based on the things you write about and how you write them, well, now that – is *content rich!*

CHAPTER REVIEW

- Blogs have taken the world by storm – writing them can be easy, fun, stress reducing – and SEO Smart!

- When you invite others to comment on what you wrote and send it on to others, you can essentially write your way to product or service buzz.

- Blogs are great vehicles for opinions, new ideas, surveys, and all types of informal, casual online conversation.

- Looking for new website content? Use your blog copy.

- Understand how tagging and keywords work with blogs – this is an important step.

- Use RSS on your Blog so users get updates as soon as they are available.

Chapter 10

PAY PER CLICK, LANDING PAGE & BANNER AD COPYWRITING

It seems that *paid* advertising will always be with us. Before the Internet, it was practically the only way to get your message out. The web was supposed to knock down a big part of this "pay for play" type of advertising mentality, but it didn't last long did it? Someone is always willing to pay for something and as long as Yahoo and Google were in control of the web and trying to do well for their shareholders, they capitalized on what became known as paid search and made it into a multi billion dollar industry. In this chapter, we discuss copy for Pay Per Click (PPC) ads, the landing page copy that these ads lead to and wrap up with a brief discussion on writing copy for banner ads. When it comes to writing copy for these important online marketing tools, there are very specific things you'll need to be aware of.

Pay Per Click – Ten Billboards in Front of Every Set of Eyes at Any Given Time

Wow, have you seen how competitive PPC advertising has been? It seems that it's working for a lot of companies out there. As you'll see for most keyword phrases that you search for, there are 8-10 PPC ads staring back at you at any given time. If you're the type of consumer who clicks on these ads, how do you choose? Some people will click on a few, others just the one that really grabs them. With all this competition, it's critical that you get the copy right. What's your headline? What's the offer? Are you a name brand or not? In the world of PPC, that doesn't really matter too much. It is interesting to see that big, well known companies are competing side by side with mom and pop online retailers. Isn't the web great?

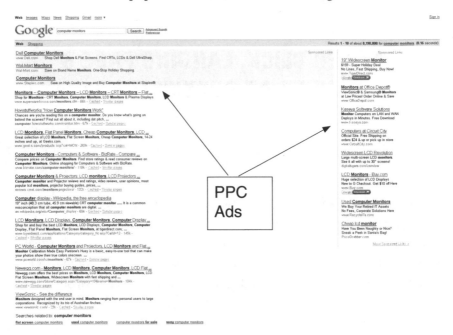

The other thing is that you have very little space for the ad itself. Every word counts with PPC! You have to make someone take some action with words that really get them motivated to click.

PPC – It's All About the Headline

Headlines are important in any ad, but they are super important in PPC ads – after all, they make up 30% or more of the total characters you are allowed to use. Plus, with 8-10 PPC ads all appearing at the same time, you need something that really pops. One of the first things you should definitely do is use your keyword phrase in the headline copy. They've searched for those words right? Well, if you deliver exactly what they are looking for, then you are potentially fulfilling their exact desire for that online shopping event. You may want to use a benefit or the company name in the headline too. Here are a couple of good examples of what you should be shooting for:

- Telegent Media – Affordable Video Montages
- SEO Website Copywriting – Industry Leader

The two keyword phrases for these headlines were "video montages" and "website copywriting." Placing them right smack dab in the middle of the headline – is a good idea.

PPC - You Need to Say A lot With Very Little Space

We know you don't have much room to sell with PPC ads. So, how do you sell it? What do you write? Once you have the headline, then you only have a couple more short lines available. You'll want to use that coveted space to write a benefit or two, what the product or service is (if you haven't said that in the headline) and a call to action.

Example PPC Ads

If you were selling GPS devices, perhaps you would go with something like this:

Dennision GPS Tracking
Reduce costs; deliver high ROI for your fleet vehicles.
Money Back Guarantee, Free Demos, find out more now!

Something like that might get someone to click. By the way, "GPS Tracking" was the keyword phrase. Of course, I've heard of companies who are totally different with their PPC ads and are looking to just stand out from all the other ones that are there among them. Some of these ads are completely irreverent, like this one for example:

Mastersons Mountain Bikes

You don't want to shop here. We don't have any of the bikes you are looking for. We offer nothing for free.

Believe it or not, some people are going to click on that ad. It may not be the exact prospect you are looking for, but it might be. Some would think it's funny, others may be curious, others look just because it's totally and utterly – different.

What's the Competition Writing?

So, what do your competitor's ads look like? It's not very hard to know – they are right there next to yours after all! You can't do that in offline advertising. With magazines and other traditional types of advertising, you don't get that luxury. I can remember flipping through dozens of magazines looking for competitive ads when I worked for a major auto manufacturer.

It's also interesting to search all your keyword phrases and see where your competitors are coming up. Some will be very aggressive and have a PPC ad for all of the available keyword phrases. Others, just a couple. So, take a look. What are they saying in their ad? What are they offering? Are they poorly written? The bad ones will really stand out. Most of them will look the same, using practically the same words. See if you can stand out and can be unique through different word choices or a more compelling offer. If you are totally stuck with the writing part, you could even use your competitors ads as inspiration to get started.

Using Price and the Word "FREE"

So are your customers price sensitive? Do they like a good value? Is your product or service a commodity? If so, and your prices are the lowest in your category (or on the lower tier compared to the competition), then placing it in the ad copy can make more people click on the ad. Your conversion numbers will probably be higher too.

And of course the word FREE. Is there another more motivating word in the English language? People are drawn to it like a magnet. If you don't have something free about your offering, *find something!* Even if it's a free white paper, you need to offer something with no strings attached. Not only is it good for PPC ads, it also makes good business sense. The word *free* has incredible power in copywriting of all types, online included.

Other ideas for this could be free shipping, buy one get one free, free 30 day trial, etc.

Credibility and Urgency – Two Important Attributes

Again, borrowing from the world of direct response advertising, you need to make sure you build some trust and get people to act now! If you have won a major award in your industry, mention it. If you have acquired a special designation or distinction that your customers will find valuable, put it into the copy. One example of this would be the 5 Star Crash Rating for automotive vehicles. If you just won it, definitely put it in there.

To get prospects to take immediate action, use copy like "ships overnight for free," or "limited availability," something like that. Using these two valuable tools can get people to click on your ad over someone else's!

PPC: Test and Measure, then Repeat

With PPC, it's all about doing it over and over again until it's perfect. When you are happy with the clicks and conversions you are getting, then you can stop changing the ad – at least for a while. You'll also want to keep your eye on the competition and monitor what they are doing. A simple headline change has been known to totally alter the click through rate of many PPC ads. Everything you write – is totally changeable. Make it right!

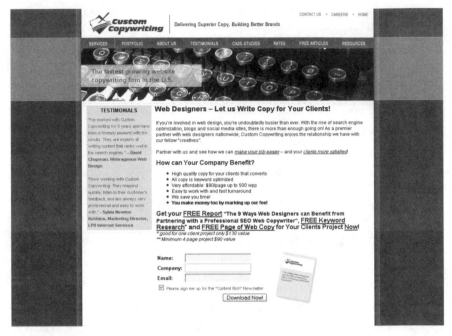

Landing Page targeted to a particular group: Web Designers

Landing Pages: Unique from your Regular Site Pages

Landing pages are what your prospects "land" on when they click on your PPC ad, banner ad or email link. With these very important pages, you have a couple of choices. You can use this page as the first and last page they interact with (i.e. Get them to take action right on that specific landing page) or as a "hub" for the other places on your site you want the prospect to go to.

I know for one company I was involved with, we had multiple elements all on one landing page: a description of key product benefits, how they compared against the competition, an icon to click on customer ROI stories, an icon to click on a product video tour, a contact form and a clickable link to download a free white paper. You don't know what that specific customer is going to want to do once they get to your site; a landing page like this gives them options. Just be careful that those other pages that they go to after the initial "hub" landing page have ways for them to contact you too – you don't want them to leave the site without doing something, which leads to this…

…What exactly are you trying to get the prospect to do? Do you want them to buy something right then and there? Or are you just trying to get their name for follow up purposes? Whatever it is you want them to do, make it *easy* for them to do it.

You only have 8-10 seconds before they leave the page – make sure your writing on that page is what they want to read.

Copy Elements on Your Landing Page that Need to Be There

Remember – it's not just about the copy. Make sure the landing page has an attractive look and feel, good use of white space, and complimentary colors. You'll want to make it a natural extension of your website's design, so in that way, it will be fairly easy. With online copy, it's always a package deal with the subsequent design.

This is Direct Marketing Folks!

You know those letters you get in the mail from credit cards, Publishers Clearinghouse and a million other companies? These letters are filled with copy and all types of emotional triggers that are trying desperately to get the reader to pick up the phone or go to a website and buy something. That's direct marketing. Your landing page copy needs to be similar. This is war after all! That hard-fought-for prospect can click back and jump on to your competitor's PPC ad after all. We can't do that with direct mail we get in our mailbox. So, basically this means writing copy that is benefits rich, offers free stuff and has a call to action.

Here is a good sample for an online radar detector retailer:

- Our SpeedPoint Radar Detection System can alert you to highway patrol within 3 miles
- Can potentially save you thousands of dollars over the next 20 years

- Can be paid for with monthly installments of only $10 with no interest accrued!
- Contact us now to schedule a FREE demo!

Not Every Landing Page Should be the Same

People are different. So are customers. You may have 30 different products that appeal to 10 very unique types of customers. It's marketing segmentation 101. So, you really need to know your prospects. How do they buy? Is it a long sales cycle or short? Do they buy spontaneously and/or immediately? Is there a certain methodology they use as they get into the buying process? If they are buying a car online, you better believe they do. Which competitor's copy are they checking out? Essentially, you'll want to create a customized landing page for that specific type of customer. If they like to know a lot before they buy, use that hub approach I discussed earlier. Through benefits rich SEO copywriting, give them all the information they need – and every chance to get in contact with you.

In addition, you may want to get with those sales people who are out pitching your product. Then bring the marketing people in too (this may be you…or the sales team and the marketing team may be just you!) and do an audit of all the copy that is being placed in the face of your prospects. You may uncover some holes in the process – and some opportunities to fix them.

If you only have one product or one service, you don't have to be as concerned with this – but you may want to do some market research anyway to see if you can uncover some things about your prospects that you may not have known. Research can uncover surprising things.

Banner/Hyperlink Copywriting

Just a quick word about banner and hyperlink copywriting. You need to be quick, concise and clear. You also need to think in terms of keywords and catch phrases. In other words, for the limited amount of space that you have, you need to be sure to do two things: use your keyword phrases in the copy and have a call to action or catch phrase (think branding) in there too.

The good thing about these types of search marketing tools is that sometimes you aren't competing with others for that same space, so you have more of the prospect's undivided attention. Maximize that opportunity!

Higher Conversion Rates with Natural Search

One final word as it relates to all this "paid copy" stuff – natural search almost always converts better. Typically, you'll get more qualified prospects too. Most people know that companies pay to be listed in the Paid listings section, it even sounds obvious, right? My company, Custom Copywriting, did PPC for four weeks back in 2003. I quickly saw that this was a complex marketing technique – and could be very expensive. I made the decision then that I would try and maximize my natural search efforts through the power of the written word, and I'm glad I did. The cost has been minimal.

I know I'm not the only one who rarely clicks on PPC ads. There's a whole group of consumers out there who feel the same way. So, basically what I'm saying is that you'll want to dedicate more time and energy on the other types of online copy creation. You'll get more long term benefit – and you won't have to pay for it.

CHAPTER REVIEW

- Pay per click (PPC) copywriting needs to be concise, keyword rich and call to action oriented.

- Make your PPC headline stand out – get them to click on it at first glance.

- Review the competitive PPC copy for tips and ideas.

- Measure PPC copy, test PPC copy and then test it again.

- Landing pages are separate from the rest of your site – make the copy there benefit rich and give them a way to get in touch with you easily.

CHAPTER 11

SEO COPYWRITING FOR EMAILS/NEWSLETTERS

Besides writing your website and all the other elements that go with it, email is your next best SEO copy "gun" in the online marketing arsenal. Written and executed poorly, email marketing can practically kill your business. Done well, and you could have SEO lightning in a bottle. Of all the copy assignments my firm has done, email is surprisingly lower on the list, but for the campaigns we have assisted with, our clients have had spectacular results. Why? There are very specific, very key things you need to consider when you write SEO copy for emails. Like your website, your job is never done. Emails are written on a regular basis; you are nurturing the relationship over time. Unlike your website, there are list considerations and customer lifecycle elements to deal with.

Whether you are emailing a newsletter, a sales promotion, a survey, an invitation or just a note to say hello, it's a big wonderful world of potential out there. So, let's get into it.

Email as a Marketing Medium

A couple of years ago, everyone was talking about all the email SPAM they received and what could be done about it. The good news is that a lot of that has been addressed. Of course, we still have an issue with junk email, but it has gotten better. So, what's the issue now? The challenge we have today is sorting through all the *relevant* emails we receive from reputable sources – things we actually want to read. It seems there's not enough time in the day.

Plus, with so many companies jumping on the bandwagon of search marketing, it seems *everyone* has a monthly newsletter they want to send you. That's both good and bad. Good, because you are getting information you requested and need to make smarter business decisions. Bad, because it's become a flood. It seems we're *drowning* in email. As time goes on, we'll learn better ways of dealing with this dynamic, for now, let's focus on how you can join the crowd and get into the email copy game!

Simply put, email is one of the most brilliant ways of communicating that human kind has ever devised. It's fast, efficient, cheap, and fairly easy, once you get the hang of it. One other thing – it can be measured. And that's the beautiful part. What better way is there to improve your writing each time around?

Define Your Goals / Audience

So, what do you want to do with your emails? Better yet, what do you want the people receiving your emails to do? Are you trying to sell something? Well, that would be a yes. Are you trying to build a relationship?

Yes.

And that's what I want to stress more than anything else. If you're old enough (I feel old just writing that), you remember getting handwritten letters. Remember that? Yeah, I know we never get them anymore. If you received them from a friend or family member, what was the goal there? Well, one of the goals was to nurture the relationship. Think of your email copy like this. Your very first email is the "Hi, my name is Jon, here is what I do and how I can help you" and every one after that is further developing that relationship. So, you'll want to write copy that reflects that approach. You'll be talking to this person over and over, again and again, even *after* they buy something from you.

So, what are your goals for the various emails you'll send out? You could be trying to build the brand. Maybe you are sending out your monthly newsletter to your customer base. Or perhaps you are sending a totally customized email to your top fifty customers? Other goals for email copy could be donation solicitation, announcing a sale, getting new leads to visit your site – there are a thousand different goals.

And then there's the audience. We'll get more into that later, but you'll want to remember who you are sending this to as you write the copy. Most people don't do that. The list that they send to is usually an afterthought. Many email campaigns are sent out to the entire house list – and everyone receives the same email. Doing this can serve a good function, but more and more, it's best to think about your customers in groups and in different stages in the relationship or "life cycle."

Copywriting for Emails – How To

It all starts with your subject line. And this is where most of the mistakes happen – right at the beginning. We all know what bad subject lines look like; we've seen enough junk email to last ten lifetimes. But how do you write your subject line so it will have maximum impact? The first thing to do is include your company name or brand. This provides instant credibility, and the spam filters will look kindly on this, especially if you consistently use this type of format on all your email campaigns. Next, use a benefit or call to action. That's right; you want to put something that will trigger interest immediately. Don't make the subject line too long. 40-60 characters should do it.

Here's a good example of a quality subject line:

Telegent Media: October Newsletter – Top 20 Tips for Lead Generation

Next is the email body. If you have written business letters before, it may come easy to you. If you haven't, there will be a learning curve. It may take multiple attempts. How to write the actual email copy? It depends on what specifically you are emailing about, but there are certain elements that they all have in common. At a basic level, make sure it has a beginning, a middle and an end. Like we discussed in an earlier chapter, use

"AIDA" – awareness, interest, desire, action. Talk about benefits and make it interactive. Many companies are now experimenting with sending video through their emails. More on that in a later chapter. Be sure to give the copy some sense of *urgency*. Whatever you are communicating, you want them to take some type of action. Use the end of the email for the big call to action piece. The "PS" is also a good place.

Finally, make sure it's clear, concise and not too "salesy." Make it personalized too. Use the customer's name. When people read their name, it's magic. Even in an email. We all like to hear or see our name.

Links and Landing Pages

So you have written some great copy for that email, but what about the interactive part? This isn't direct mail baby! People are going to be doing things as they read or scan the email you sent them. In any email, there could be as few as one link to one landing page, or as many as ten or more. This can be pretty complex! The main emphasis here is that you do in fact think in terms of the email being a conversation you would have on the phone with a customer. After you say something, you want them to say (or do something) – like click on a link for example and sign up for your white paper, or take a demo of the product.

Be sure to measure the activity your links inspire. You'll find some that hardly anyone clicks on, and others you thought may not have been as interesting, clicked on the most. It's always interesting to see what happens when people open up the email. What's their behavior going to be like?

Be sure to make your email a very *interactive* experience. Anything less can inspire no action. Very uninspiring.

Choosing an Email Vendor

If you are a rookie, this may be a new thing for you. If you think you're going to send the emails out from your personal email account, you are mistaken. There is way too much you'd have to do to manage that process to make it worthwhile. An email vendor will automate the entire process for you, including developing the content, picking the list,

Common Problems

There are quite a few when it comes to email copywriting:

- Don't forget the Call to Action. Your recipients must have a way to get in touch with you. Make it obvious: use a button or a link – or use both.

- Be sure to include your phone number and if you are a local business, your physical address so people who want to contact you in other ways can do so. Remember, not everyone likes email.

- Make the form they'll need to fill out on the landing page simple. You only have their attention for a few seconds.

- Place the most important content of the email "above the fold" – in other words, above where they'll need to scroll on the screen.

- Use the right email list or database! This is probably the number one most common problem. The wrong group gets the wrong message. Oops!

- Make it very easy to unsubscribe. This is one of my pet peeves. What's up with the maze of instructions to stop getting the email? One click, and you're done. That's how it should be.

sending the emails out, and maybe most important, providing you with the analysis report of who opened the email, when and what they did when they read it. Did they click on a certain link? You'll know.

There are at least twenty good email marketing vendors. The names you hear a lot are Constant Contact, Vertical Response, and Yes Mail[40].

They all have their pluses and minuses, and certain ones will appeal to certain types of personalities. If you are just getting into email writing and marketing, take a spin on a few and see what you like. Sign up for a free trial. I did this recently with a new vendor and was really happy with what I saw. Lots of good stuff out there!

Is Your List Right?

It may seem obvious, but it needs to be brought up. Who are you sending all these well-crafted emails to? Are you sending to those who have voluntarily subscribed through a double opt in process or are you buying a list? Maybe you are doing both. Word to the wise: buying or renting an email list can be problematic. You may have some issues with spam accusations, etc. Plus, do you really know much about this "list" of so called "prospects?" Lots of money has been made by list vendors – both good and bad ones – because this part of the process was botched up pretty badly by the email marketer.

A list will need to be managed. Peoples' email addresses change all the time. Their interests may change. They may edit their preferences of how and when they want to be contacted. Like a good bottle of wine, an email list is a *living thing*, and it needs to be nurtured. Be sure to make this a priority. It's just as important as writing the copy.

Write the Copy Anytime – But Choose When you Send It

You can write your emails at 3:00 am if you like. OK, that's not going to happen, but the point is that *when* you write is not very important. Of course, if you are a morning person, choosing to write then would probably be good. The key here is *the time you send the email.* When you get it to them is important. Your goal is to get 100% of your recipients to open that beautiful prose you wrote. Knowing that, you'll want to send your emails out in the middle of the day – send it in the morning, and you'll get buried among all the other emails that typically go out during this busy period.

Send it in the evening, or even later in the day, and you'll get people who are tired and want to go home. When they come back the next morning, they will have forgotten about your email. In addition, don't send it out on Monday. Sending it on Tuesday, Wednesday or Thursday works better.

How is Email Copywriting Different from Traditional Sales Letters and Direct Mail?

With email, you are a needle in a haystack. At least with direct mail, you'll have your place among just a few other items in the mailbox – and you probably have a better chance of being opened too. Of course, if you are emailing your customer base and especially if those individuals have opted into your email, you're much better off. Many of these folks will look forward to receiving your email newsletter, offer or announcement. But if you are emailing a new list, take this advice to heart.

First, the good things about email copy: (besides it being very inexpensive)

- **Hyperlinks** – they can lead right to a customized landing page, right into your site and give the prospect an opportunity to find out more or purchase right then and there. They have to call or take an extra step to log on to your site with direct mail.

- Second, you can **customize the copy** directly to a certain group of customers – or even an individual customer. That can be very powerful.

- Last, **you can interact with them as they open the email** if you like through a live chat or instant messenger feature. Some people will like this, others will not, but it's definitely a huge advantage over traditional sales letters and direct mail.

A Word About Attachments

You can't use attachments with the large email marketing vendors out there. This is due to all of the SPAM problems over the past few years. The way around this? Simply embed links for whatever document you want to attach and host the document on your site. Whether it's an order form, a spreadsheet, a promotional flyer, coupons or anything else, this fix will work perfectly, plus it gets them onto your site.

Different Customer Groups Need Different Emails

If you run a car dealership, do you think a guy who just bought a car from you should get the same email as the gal who is just curious about the models you offer? How about the regular lifelong department store customer who has been shopping at the same place for 30 years, the person who knows everyone's name at the store, should you write the same email copy to this person as you would for someone who just filled out the catalog request form? The answers here are obvious, and I think you get the point. The problem is that very few companies think about their email copy in this way. Tailor your messages to specific customer groups! The loyal customer should get more (and better) offers than the infrequent one.

Another good trick is to ask those people who are signing up to receive your email newsletter a few simple questions. When you do this, you'll get a good understanding of the person's psychographics. Allow them to select their areas of interest. A subscriber could indicate their job title or function. They could check what types of email communications they want, whether it be upcoming sales, newsletters, or other. They could also tell you what products or services they are interested in ahead of time. Once you know this type of information, you are set to write a specific email customized especially for them!

Special Considerations for Newsletters

If you don't have a newsletter or a newsletter sign up on your website, you have to get one. Today! You have a golden opportunity to throw a personalized paper right on the doorstep of every customer and prospect you have in your database! More than this, you have the ability to place that morning "paper" right on their office desk. Wow, newspapers would have loved that back in the pre-Internet days, right?

What are some of the other special points about writing newsletter copy?

- You want to include many different types of content in the body of the newsletter: articles, surveys, promos, research findings, simple case studies, links to multiple landing pages on your site. It's all good.

- The way it *looks* is really important. Work closely with your graphic designer, web designer or automated email marketing vendor to ensure it looks good before it goes out. You don't want to look amateur.

- Make it easy for them to forward to a friend or bring another party into the fray. Leverage the viral aspect. A good newsletter with lots of subscribers can be very powerful, especially to those who are receiving it for the first time. I know I've considered signing up for online marketing newsletters simply because they had thousands of people reading them.

Don't Forget About These...

There are other things you'll want to keep in mind with your email copywriting. For example, have you checked to make sure the links are working? Have you done some testing, sending the email to yourself (and a couple other people...more eyes are always better) in both HTML and text versions? Like your web pages, is there a good balance between design/

graphics and the copy itself? Do you have some good white space in there? The copy is critical, but so is the rest.

Finally, there is this: what's going to happen if you send out your email to 1,000 people and you get 250 email replies? Who is receiving the emails and completed contact us forms you get back? How are you following up? The writing doesn't stop after you write the first email – it goes on into perpetuity! You're going to learn to love to write! Seriously though, this is an important consideration. Getting a 25% response rate would be HUGE – but it does happen. Just make sure something positive happens on your end if the customer or prospect raises their hand and says "Yes, count me in!"

CHAPTER REVIEW

- Email marketing has changed a lot over the past few years, but email copywriting hasn't - connect with specific customers, offer them valuable information, nurture the relationship and lead them to the sale.

- Include your company name or newsletter title in the subject line so you don't end up in the Spam filter.

- Use the right list of contacts and select a reputable email marketing vendor.

- A newsletter is a unique email marketing medium. Make it engaging with lots of different types of content: articles, surveys, promos, case studies, etc.

REAL WORLD SEO COPYWRITING EXAMPLES & THE REST

Part III

CHAPTER 12

SEO COPYWRITING FOR SMALL/MEDIUM SIZED BUSINESSES

If you have a small to medium-sized business, being on the web is absolutely essential to your success. In fact, it could be the best thing you ever did, or better yet – the driving force that is making a real difference in how you compete.

Most new businesses that become small to medium-sized companies are savvy enough to go to the web first. Let's face it, of all the new businesses out there, virtual companies or *e-commerce* sites are the fastest growing. But if you own a bakery, a restaurant or a computer equipment store; a "brick and mortar" business, you'll want to have a web presence as well and then build content – intelligently and consistently so you can *"write yourself to wealth"* just like the other guys. Remember, local search is a big deal – and will continue to be a big factor (More on that later in the chapter). Let's say you own an Italian restaurant in Stockton, California. When Mrs. Jones is looking for a great restaurant to take her in-laws to, you want to make sure you are on the first page of the results when she types "Italian restaurant in Stockton" in a Google search!

Of all the companies I work with, 80% of them are small to medium sized firms. Ever since Ronald Reagan led the small business revolution twenty five years ago, it has been a "mom and pop" dominated landscape. That's a great thing – but you know what? A majority of those companies, maybe even a few who are reading this book right now – could do a whole lot more to maximize their web content and bring more sales in the door. Why aren't these businesses doing more writing on their websites and through other online channels? Some of these folks would say they are too busy. Others think they have maximized what can be done online. A few don't care. The rest are probably "old school" in their approach – they just don't get it.

Perhaps one is an industrial machine manufacturer, like a company I worked with two months ago. This particular company had been around for 50 years and never had more than a badly designed home page with a couple of sentences of copy. Within a week, they had 15 pages of new, fresh content that explained who they were, what they did and how they could help their customers. A partner firm I was working with on the project even started a link building program for them. A blog? Probably not the right thing for them. But it would be for many other companies.

One other thing – there are many large, multi-national companies out there that are spending millions on traditional advertising campaigns, like TV and radio, but forget entirely about the web! And we are talking big names. This is especially true for new segments and trendy niches. As a smaller company, this is a giant opportunity.

So, what can you do with web content if you are a small to medium sized business? What are the opportunities and what do you need to know? How can you use web content as an effective business strategy – or integrate it into current tactics and strategies? Let's find out.

Compete with the Big Guys for Search Engine Real Estate

Good news! You can compete with the big guys for search engine real estate. There are so many examples of this, it really is mind blowing. So let me ask you a question: when has this opportunity ever occurred? If you answered never, you would be correct. If you don't think you can *write your way to wealth* on the web as a small business, you are absolutely dead wrong! You can. To be honest, I was a little surprised when I had the ability to gain such an enviable spot in the online copywriting space in such a short amount of time. Where were all the traditional advertising agencies? Where were the digital advertising agencies? No where.

How was I able to gain a foothold online in the copywriting space when there are literally thousands of agencies out there that had been writing copy for decades? Because the web is a democracy in many ways – it's open for almost anyone who has a good idea, to do a few certain things right and capture market share. Of course, there are lots of factors at work: the Internet is growing like crazy, there's enough work out there for everyone, the agencies may not want the business, etc. But, the point is that *it can be done.*

The other thing is that many people would prefer to do business with a small to medium sized business rather than a big corporation. If you personally write your articles, author your blog, write your site content and put together a few white papers and newsletters, then there's only one thing that potential clients could say: you are an expert! The issue really is this: not every small to medium sized business knows what to do on the web from a copywriting perspective to make the good things happen. Of course, the other thing is that they have always heard that advertising costs money. You have to spend money to make money. Hmmm, that's funny. I didn't spend any money on advertising last month! And I'm talking about the new clients. If this book doesn't tell you how to do it, then I'm missing the mark. Yes, I know I'm biased – but I *know* it will.

The only thing separating your business from competing with the big guys and winning is a little hard work and persistence. Start writing your way *today.*

Content Approval is Easy

Isn't is great to have your own business and not have to get approval from an endless hierarchy of executives? This may be the biggest benefit of all. Without naming any names, I have worked for companies in the past (And you probably have too) where I had written a sales letter or web page that had to go through ten cycles of review, from five different people who all had different opinions of what it should look like. Is this the copywriter's hell? I vote for yes on that one. Meanwhile, while you're going though all those cycles of revisions, the competition has already met the customer need and is fast at work gaining their business and their loyalty.

The other point is that you don't have to worry about the IT and Marketing departments agreeing. This can be close to impossible in many cases. Why? Because they see the world through different eyes. If you are the marketer, you want to fully explain the features and benefits, and you may want to use a little bit of flowery imagery to do it. The engineer or webmaster? They want just the facts. They're thinking of systems and how things work. Not all of the time, of course, but it's definitely an issue that I have seen personally many times. If you are a medium sized business, you may still have to deal with this, but it will be a lot easier because you only have one guy in Marketing (you) and one gal in IT. That's not bad. It makes things a lot easier.

Looking Big When You're Tiny

Being virtual has incredible advantages, right? Even when my company was tiny, you couldn't tell by my website. I looked big. Why? Content. Lots of site content and lots of links pointing back to my site because of articles I had written (and for other reasons). Think about it – how many sites have you seen that had page after page of great content; white papers and newsletter archives, online articles and pages for every product or service and then found out somehow that it was operated by one guy from his apartment in Cleveland? There are thousands of sites like this all over the world.

The bottom line is that people want to feel they are dealing with a reputable organization that knows what it is doing. They really don't decide to go with your small business because you look *big* necessarily; they just want to feel confident that they will get what they pay for. All those pages of content that you write will have a positive effect on your business – in ways that you can't even begin to imagine. You're going to get calls from all kinds of companies that you never thought you would have the benefit of working with.

After all, when you start a company and start writing online content, you don't really know what business you are going to be in. Your customers will tell you that, over time. I got into this business because I liked to write, plain and simple. I thought I would be writing ad copy, direct mail copy and other traditional copywriting type projects. A year into my business, guess what I was doing? Hardly any of the above, but tons of web copy, email content and online articles. Within two years, much to my amazement, I was getting these types of requests:

"Do you do web site design?"

"Can you also design my ad for me?"

"Do you guys also take care of the site's monthly SEO?"

"How about distribution of the articles? Can I pay you to do this too?"

The answers to all of them were YES! Of course we do that!

Pretty soon, you won't just look big when you're tiny. You will most definitely, certifiably be big – or on your way to being big. That's the way it goes on the web. You simply have to dust that computer keyboard off and start the writing!

Using Blogs, Press Releases and Articles to Fast Track Growth

There's no doubt about it, blogs are everywhere. Who would have thought that a vast collection of "online journals" filled with thoughts, opinions and ideas would have been almost as big of a revolution as the web itself! The fact is that it has and you can definitely use it to your advantage. Remember what I said in the Introduction of this book? I commented on the fact that writing is going through its second revolution – the first being driven by the printing press. This one is being driven by the rise of the web. Like those early publishers that took advantage of the press, you can take advantage of the web to become a serious player. How successful do you want to be? The sky is the limit.

Don't let the "blog mob" take you over however! Don't start writing one just to have one, and don't think that's all you have to do – or can do to make your small or medium sized business stand out. Get on those press releases and articles too! Use the releases to announce important company events, product launches and service notices. Use article writing to gain valuable, free online exposure. For more information on these specific seo copywriting strategies, take a look at the individual chapters in this book that discuss each one.

Keep Growing Your Content

Your content is never finished. Don't forget that! I know how easy it is to forget about it. I have made the mistake myself. I have, without a doubt, missed out on business opportunities that I could have had. I realize that. The good thing is that you can always pick up where you left off. If you haven't updated your site for a few months, simply take a look at where you could build out the content and start brainstorming ideas. Put together an outline of what you could write in the new space and when you are ready, begin writing.

If you are not sure what to do to build new content, check out your competitor's websites. What are they doing? How does your site compare? Go on to LinkPopularity.com and see what articles or press releases they have out there. Doing this will definitely give you a ton of ideas. If you hit a wall, simply use the same angle/topic they have used and translate it into your own experience. If they wrote a "top 10 ways my clients benefit from my service," do the same thing for your site!

The other great thing about growing your content and continuing to write, write, write is that the search engines love it. You will absolutely, without a doubt, get a boost in search engine rankings when you make a commitment to write more and follow through with it. If you are a small online retailer or mid-sized manufacturer with a web presence, this is a fantastic way to go up against larger competitors and win every time. You can and will out-write them!

Get a Basic Site Up in a Week!

If you are one of the thousands (yes there are many) who still don't have a web presence and haven't written any search engine optimized web copy – there is always time to start. After all, you can get a site up in a week. You wouldn't be able to do that if you were larger, a big Corporation for example, but you can as a smaller firm. All you need to start is seven to eight pages – a Home page, About Us, Product or Service pages, FAQ, Why Use Us? And a Contact Us page. After this, you can expand a million different ways, but that is all you need to get in the game.

The first step would be to find a good web designer who won't charge you a fortune – and who specializes in designing for small business. There are hundreds of good web designers out there. But be sure they know SEO. There are many who don't. Now that you know everything you need to know about SEO copywriting, you can approach them with some good, solid knowledge. When you talk with them, be sure you let them know that you understand what SEO is about, at least from a copywriting point of view. You can get a good basic site designed for $2000 or less. Don't believe anyone who tells you otherwise!

If you need to bring on a writer, then do it. Don't struggle through it if you honestly can't, (or don't want to) write. It will be a sound investment.

Profile: A Good Example of Small Business Web Content Success

There's nothing like taking a look at some good examples. One of the things I do when I'm writing for an industry that is totally new to me is search the keywords and take a look at a few competitors' sites. It can be very revealing to see what others are up to. You can stack up the competition, see where the opportunities may be and find out where you may fit into the mix. I recommend it for any new, small or mid sized company trying to find new opportunities.

Over the past few years, I've worked with a bunch of small companies that would be great examples of what to strive for with your web content. Unfortunately, I couldn't get all of them to agree to be profiled in the book, but I did happen to find a couple of great ones.

Here is a before and after image of a Home page for Provada, an insurance services provider, with the new items pointed out. Interesting, huh?

BEFORE:

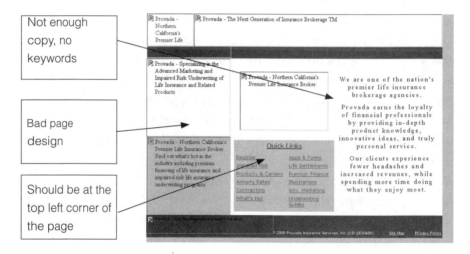

AFTER:

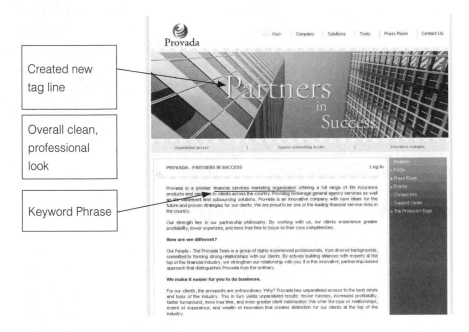

Created new tag line

Overall clean, professional look

Keyword Phrase

Maximize the Power of Local Search

We cover local search in depth in our "Future of SEO Copywriting" chapter coming up, but wanted to touch on it here as well because it applies almost entirely to small and mid sized businesses.

So, first of all, what is it? *Local search* is a relatively new SEO and Search Marketing concept that is severely underutilized and unknown. Essentially, it's the way local, neighborhood businesses are found on the web. Let's say you have a small electronics store in Toledo, Ohio. Historically, you have always relied on people driving by and seeing your store, and coming in because they know where you are located. Or, you have just serviced existing customers and never thought of expanding your business to the web. You may not even *have* a website.

But what about those people who have never been to your store, don't know where you are located and are looking for an electronics store in Toledo on the web? If they type in "electronics store + Toledo," local search would place your company right at the top of those search results. That guy could check out your site and buy something without ever leaving his house. You get the order and ship it off to him. He pays right on your site and you put that money in the bank!

How is Local Search impacting businesses? It is bringing in whole new revenue streams! It's changing the very way we shop and buy goods and services in our communities! It's a revolution! Local Search will only continue to grow and prosper. If you ask me, I am shocked that it took this long to really catch on. When I first found out about the web in 1995 or so, it was one of the first things I thought about. Wow, this could make a real impact on little retailers. Well, it has finally.

Major pundits are saying that the web will influence a *trillion* dollars of off-line local spending within three to four years.[41] Yes, that's <u>trillion.</u>

How do you get in on the action of local search? Well, first of all, if you don't have a website, you'll need one as soon as possible. That's a given. Next, you'll need to optimize your copy as I have explained in this book. You'll also need to optimize the site – make sure you use a web designer who knows SEO. Make sure you have used all your keyword terms plus the local cities and geographic words. This is absolutely critical to being found.

If you do pizza delivery, focus on your prices, specials and fast delivery in your copywriting. If you are a plumber or pest control business, your copywriting should reflect your 24/7 availability and customer satisfaction.

Focusing on what's most important to your local audience will serve you very well.

Once you are benefiting from local search, be sure to analyze the traffic you are getting. If you need to tweak a few things in the copy or add some more pages to your site, do it. Local search could change the very way you do business.

 Partner with Users, Customers and Others for Content

Consider this question: are you asking every customer for a testimonial? If you aren't, well then this is a huge chance that you are missing. What about case study opportunities? Writing about how you took a client from nothing to something and then getting the word out there is *very* powerful. All in all, these two very important areas of web content are critical. I know for us, it has made a big difference. We have a page on our site dedicated to customer testimonials. We also have a page for case studies. These two pages have brought us customers we never thought we would have had the chance to work with.

Why? There's just something magical about third party validation. People trust it. For most of ours, we even include the person's full name and company information so potential customers can call the company directly and ask them what they thought of our service. How many businesses can you do that with? Not enough. Wouldn't you love to talk to ten people about a prospective doctor you are considering? Sure would be nice! Well, you can utilize this type of content on your site *today* so that you can start getting new customers through it tomorrow.

A case study is a "testimonial on steroids." Most prospective customers who read a few of these on your site are sold after they understand how you impacted a company like theirs. Think about it: you aren't really even writing the content! With a testimonial, you're asking for their opinion. They jot down a few lines, email it to you and you place it on your site. Simple as that. All you have to do is grab your customer list and shoot them an email. What do you say? Here's how we word it:

Bob,

Just wanted to drop you a line to thank you again for your business! We really enjoyed working with you and hope that the content we wrote for your site is working well. With every client we work with, we like to ask for a review of how we did. Would you mind taking a moment to write up a testimonial for us? We like to post these on our site to let other prospective customers know what we could do for them. I really appreciate your help with this – thanks again!

Jon Wuebben
Custom Copywriting

And that's pretty much it. Within a week, you could have a whole new batch of great content to put up on your site. Case study requests take a little longer, and they do require you to do a little writing, but they are well worth the effort. You'll want to hand pick just the best customers with the best stories to tell – and you may have to go through quite a few to get a few good ones, but again, it's a world class way to make your site content rich!

Other ways you can get users or customers to help with content is through blogs and forums, which we covered in depth in other chapters.

Write Your Own Product/Service Reviews

Get on Amazon and Ebay and start writing your own reviews of products and/or services related to your business. Example: Find all the books that apply to what you do, read them and then post reviews. Most sites allow you to create a profile, where you can even include your business website URL! How's that for a nice link to your site from a big site? You also get a little extra promotion for you and your company!

B2B vs B2C

B2B	B2C
more service based	more product based
brand ID created through personal relationships	brand ID created through repetition, imagery and emotional appeal
focuses on awareness building	focuses on merchandising, special offers, discounts
buying decision based on rational decision, made by consensus based on business value	buying decision is an emotional decision, based on status, price

B2B or B2C – The Differences in Copywriting Techniques

Who do you sell to? Consumers or other businesses? There are many differences in how B2B and B2C companies operate; but we'll save that complete discussion for another book. What we want to ascertain here are the communication and copywriting differences for these unique audiences. First, the similarities: they *both* are interested in something that you have to sell, they *both* want to know what's in it for them and how much the product or service costs. *Both* types of audiences research and buy online. The differences really come in to play in *how* they do all of the above.

The first major distinction is that they typically have a different sales cycle. B2B buys slower and it's more of a relationship thing. Many companies are looking for a long term partnership, so they will research quite a few firms over a long period of time before they buy. Copywriting here needs to be reflective of this – no quick sale, "buy now" jargon. Next are the differences between services and products. B2B is more service based and B2C sells more products. How you "sell" services in the copy would speak more to the technical support that's offered, how much consultant's time they have available on the contract, etc. Product copywriting is more feature/benefit and call to action based.

What types of copy would a B2B client respond better to? Probably more fact based, more executive summary type of information. If a company is comparing business software providers and they are looking through forty companies, they want quick details communicated. They don't have a lot of time.

With B2B, brand identity is created and sustained through personal relationships, with B2C; it's generated through repetition, imagery and emotional appeal. B2B focuses on awareness building and showing why they are better than competitor X. With B2C, it's all about merchandising, special offers, discounts (sometimes) and point of purchase displays. And that leads right into the last major difference: how the buying decision is made. B2B is typically a rational decision, made by consensus based on the business value. B2C is many times an emotional one, based on status, expectations of what the product can do for them and/or price.

What's also interesting is that B2B companies, as a whole, don't embrace search marketing as much as you would think. Trade shows, public relations, direct mail and print advertising are all utilized more. If you are B2B, you can beat your competitors online by knowing this and taking advantage of the opportunity. Start writing now!

CHAPTER REVIEW

- Smaller companies can compete very effectively on the web against the bigger guys – maximize the opportunity.

- Unlike corporations, content approval is easy; leverage your ability to move quickly in the face of competition.

- If you are a tiny firm operating from your home, copywriting can make you look big, providing you with the image and credibility you need.

- If you want to turn your small company into a large corporation in the shortest amount of time, use blog, press release and article copy to take you there.

- Repeat this three times fast: I will continue to grow my content; I will continue to grow my content, I WILL CONTINUE TO GROW MY CONTENT!

- If you are a small hometown company, get to know Local Search – it can revolutionize your business.

- Partner with everyone – users, customers or internal staff for content.

CHAPTER 13

SEO COPYWRITING FOR LARGER CORPORATIONS

Think it's easy for a corporation to build out content on their website? Guess again. It's the toughest of all – but if you are a Fortune 100 Marketing Manager or Director of Online Marketing for a major corporation, there are tips and tricks to help get you there faster – and more successfully.

Let's face it; this can be really complex with all the factors that are out there to manage through. There's the budget process, business unit objectives, confusing channel strategies, integration with PR and traditional advertising and many more. Corporations have a tough copywriting row to hoe.

I was recently at Search Engine Strategies in San Jose, the most popular conference in the industry. It was interesting hearing the feedback from all the corporate attendees that were there. It's very different from what you hear with the web startups and other small businesses. First, many of them don't know the first thing about how to write their sites. Second, many of them have always outsourced that function. Then there's the whole culture clash between IT and Marketing that you hear about – how do you get things approved? You find out that things move a lot slower on the corporate side of the fence – for a good reason. There are ways around all of this however, so let's get into it.

Keyword Research is Critical

If you have 300 products, broken out into 20 product categories, with 10 locations across the country, you are going to have a few keyword phrases to be concerned with. The fact is, you are probably missing out on a bunch of keyword phrases. If I was the head of a large company and wanted to increase my online marketing efforts, it would be the first place I'd look. There are countless stories out there of corporations that went though an extensive keyword research process, only to find out they were missing out on 10-20% of the ones their competitors, or customers were using.

This can be an expensive or inexpensive process depending on budgets, needs, timing and other considerations. Expensive if you contract with a Search Marketing firm and have them do it for you. What's the inexpensive route? Talk to customers, check your log files, look at the competitors' sites. Get a free trial to www.WordTracker.com or www.Keyword-Discovery.com and see what they come up with. You will be surprised. But you'll also be excited because you'll see right away that those missing keywords could mean more online sales or lead opportunities.

Another way to get on top of your keyword situation is to get a good analytics program and see what it's telling you. If I was working at a major corporation and had responsibility for online marketing, I would try out a couple different providers through a free trial, just like with the keyword research sites. Not sure which one to try? www.Clicktracks.com and www.WebTrends.com are both great. See what they offer and take advantage of this opportunity!

Getting your keywords right could mean the difference between just doing okay on the web and explosive, forever growing online sales!

Ensure All Worldwide Sites are Speaking the Same Language

I don't mean that literally. The copy on your sites across the globe should be in whatever language is required based on country. What I mean is that running an entire fleet of websites and managing the copy can be a very complex task. You want to make sure that whatever features and benefits you have on your American site are also on your French site and your Chinese site, translated correctly based on cultural differences as well. Don't make the same advertising mistake that a few large Fortune 100 companies did in the 60s, 70s and even the 80's did. What did they do? Well, it's what they *didn't do* that was really the issue. If the ad copy says "Our Cars will Make Feel Powerful," it should be translated into the same thing in the other language (if it translates that is).

So, how can you best go about making sure your sites are congruent, that there are no discrepancies or oversights? Take an audit. Go through and check them out, side by side, page by page. You'll need to do it with someone who speaks the other country's language. This will also help you find other content opportunities. Your German site may have ten pages dedicated to articles on topics that would be interesting to customers there, but you may have forgotten to include this section on your British site. Or, you may have built out additional product content that discussed real users' experiences or case studies but failed to do that on all your online properties. Whatever the case may be, use this opportunity as a way to improve the content on all of your sites.

One other point on this topic: you DO want to make your unique worldwide sites different, based on the customers' needs in those geographies. You don't want to make everything the same – far from it. You just want to be aware that major problems could come up if you have content on one site that doesn't match up with content from another site. By the way, this is also true for different divisions or business units within a company. And this may be easier to miss because the different entities may not communicate much. If this is the case for you, be sure to reach out to your counterpart.

There's one thing I missed – how about those companies that have one site with a language selector on the splash or home page? Well, it's easier to audit, but all the rules and recommendations above still apply. This will be the case with many global, multi-national companies.

Copywriting and Design: In House or Outsourced?

Having seen this issue up close and personal at a few different corporations, I'm going to take a stand on the second half of this one and recommend outsourcing the web design. Why? The biggest benefit is that an outside agency can be very objective. You definitely need this when you are considering your web design. Plus, most in house graphic designers that I have come across over the years don't know Search Engine Optimization (SEO) at all. You can't have this! It's critical to the entire process.

As far as copywriting is concerned, well, you have this book, right? You have all you need to write web copy effectively! If you feel like you don't, then just email me. I'll answer whatever additional questions you may have (See my contact info in the back). Seriously, most corporations have fairly large marketing departments, with a few copywriters on staff, or at least an Administrator or two who writes sales letters and other marketing materials. These folks can write your web copy too, they'll just need to be sure to work closely with the site designers or Search Marketing firm you choose.

For some corporations, budget will be an issue. That's just a reality of corporate life. Politics may be an issue too. That's a whole different subject altogether, and outside the scope of this book, but just know that it could be a factor. For the money part, you'll naturally have to do things in-house if this is a concern. However, with the right designer and copywriter working in synergy – it could be a match made in heaven! I've seen this happen.

Getting IT and Marketing to Agree

Who manages the company website? Well, that's a great question. Most corporations wouldn't have a great answer to that one. IT manages updates, does all the coding and takes care of any server problems, etc. Marketing writes the copy and designs the site. But here is the problem: the website is a vehicle for sales and public awareness. Changes have to be made all the time based on keyword research and/or competitors' moves. As a Marketer, you need to make those changes fast and efficiently. But IT has 23 other projects ahead of yours. They also may flat out disagree with you on how the site needs to be changed.

The other critical piece is the META tags. Who writes those? IT or Marketing? THIS SHOULD ALWAYS BE A MARKETING TASK! I stress that because it's one of the most important take aways from this chapter. The title and description tags are super important. You'll want to put your keywords in there for sure, and you'll want every page's META tags to be unique. More on that next. Don't let the IT Department have their way with this one. You will pay for it with big missed opportunities.

The way to get IT and Marketing to agree is to find some middle ground. "I'll do this for you to make your life simpler and you'll do this for me to make my life simpler" is the idea. Of course, having an honest discussion about your ideas and the online opportunities is a good idea too. If communicating becomes a problem, as it might between two very different groups of people like IT and Marketing, then the best thing to do would be to involve upper management as soon as possible.

Don't Forget the META Tag Copy

Do you know how many corporations miss the META tag copy? A ton of them. Having been at a couple of Search Engine Strategy Conferences, I've seen this as one of the biggest eye openers for corporate attendees. They don't realize how important it is. So let's break it down. What are they, what can you do to manage them and why are they important? Well, we covered them in an earlier chapter, but they are so important, we'll discuss again...

The META tags are part of the back end coding of the site that directly influence your search engine rankings. There are three that are important: the Title tag, Description tag and Keywords tag. Actually, the Keywords tag isn't that important anymore, but the other two definitely are. You'll see title tags for web pages at the very top of the page when you are online.

The meta tags I recently wrote for a Foreclosure website's home page:

The title tag:

FORECLOSURE SOFTWARE I FORECLOSED HOMES I FORECLOSURE LISTINGS

The description tag:

"XYZ Company provides foreclosure software, e-commerce marketing and foreclosure training solutions for those who provide foreclosure listings as well as real estate professionals; our team has many years experience in the foreclosed homes industry."

So basically the tags tell the search engines (and people) what your site is about. It's also a place that you'll want to use your keywords – the specific ones you are using for that page that is. Mix them in; don't make it sound like it would if you used keyword phrases too much. Meta tags are also important because it's an easy way to get a leg up on your competitors who aren't paying attention to it. If you want to check them out on your site, simply go on to a page, right click and select "View Page Source." You'll see a bunch of code come up in a window. The META tags are pretty obvious – they will say "TITLE," "DESCRIPTION" AND "KEYWORD." You can't miss them. Of course, if your pages don't have them at all – then this represents an even bigger opportunity.

Watch Out for the Little Guy Taking Search Engine Market Share!

In every industry around the world, there are little companies literally taking online market share away from larger companies that should almost have a right to it. Ever heard of Zappos.com[42]? A few years ago, they were non-existent. Today, they are the largest online shoe retailer in the world. How did that happen? Well, it happened because there were some very large, well known shoe retailers that took their eye off the ball. We won't name any names, but maybe they didn't think that the online space would be very big.

If you are working for a large corporation, take a look at which other companies are coming up for your keyword phrases. Are there any you've never heard of? There will probably be a few. If so, do what you can *quickly* to turn this around. I emphasize the word quickly because this is one of the reasons they were able to get high up in the search rankings to begin with. As a smaller company, they can move fast. If you think you can just avoid this issue and pretend it will go away – or think it's not important, I hate to say it, but you are wrong. It's like the opposite of the Wal-Mart effect. This is a "smaller company dominating larger company" thing!

Get Away from the Dreaded "Corporate Speak"

This is the dread of all those who know how to write or appreciate good writing! It's called Corporate Speak. You know what it is; you're on a site and they basically say something like this:

Accme Corp distributes a diversified product mix, including chemicals, equipment and instruments, furniture, protective apparel, production and safety products, and other laboratory products and supplies.

Accme Corp supports its customers by providing storeroom management, product procurement, supply chain integration, technical expertise and laboratory consulting.

Accme Corp maintains operations in over 60 countries and employs over 50,000 people around the globe. Accme Corp is headquartered in Miami, Florida.

Looking at the above example of "corporate speak", what does that mean exactly? Is that the way people communicate in real life? No. Is this the type of copy that resonates with people? No. Unfortunately, content like this is found all over the web on lots of company websites. I think its origins are pre-baby boomer; it reminds me of something I would have read from the 1960's – that's how out of date this stuff is! You can almost hear them saying, *"We have to sound official and big and like we are the solution to all needs"*... no, actually it makes a company sound distant and un-human. It doesn't communicate what the corporation actually does, how they add value to someone's life and what the features and benefits are of their products or services.

The better way to write copy – whether you are a corporation or not, is to write in a *conversational* way.

"But we won't sound official and corporate," you say. Well, maybe you need to take a step back and realize first how much things have changed in business. People don't care about that anymore. Consumers want *good value* and *great service*. They really don't care that you are official and corporate. So, instead of writing you "provide solutions for the marine and boating market," say this: "Are you in the market for a new boat? Johnson Marine Products sells the highest quality sail boats in the industry." It just communicates *better.* And that's what we are trying to do, right?

If you want to be a little "corporate" and sound "polished" – which is what defenders of this type of copy would say – save it for your brochures and other printed material. A good idea would be to mix this type of copy with the more casual, conversational type. Doing this will give good contrast, as long as it all works together.

Copywriting for Lead Generation

With small companies, lead generation is important, but with corporations, it takes on a life of its own. Not only is it critical to the overall business strategy, whatever that might be, but it can be a complex activity, managed by an entire team of people. Speaking of strategy – what's your strategy for lead generation copywriting? The words you use are a very big part of the whole process. Well, because we are talking about online copy, let's talk about the online vehicles for lead generation. They are all covered in depth as individual chapters in this book, but in order of importance, they are website, email, pay per click, newsletter and article. Blogs are newer and not totally adopted by business in a major way yet, but if implemented correctly with a wide user base, they could be the most important for lead generation.

We'll cut to the chase with this one and then break it down into its core elements:

Consumers have changed over the past couple of generations. They can't be sold to – they <u>buy from you</u>. With lead generation copy, you need to use language that provides them with something of value for free first and work consciously to build the relationship with them, ultimately selling them something (And then selling them again and again because you have had the goal to create a relationship from the very start).

How does this impact the copy and the vehicles that will deliver the copy? On your website, you want to have multiple places where they can contact you. You'll want to have videos on your site that explain the product or service.

Copy idea: *"Listen to Company President Bob Matthews talk about how BriteStar has helped service providers like you save 50% on their monthly fees and better communicate with their customers!"*

You'll want to offer a free trial (service) or free sample (product).

Copy idea: *"Curious how Telegent Media could improve your online analytics measurement? Try it for a week for FREE and see! No commitment and no credit card required."*

You'll want to have white papers that explain more.

Copy idea: *"Our white paper on utilizing GPS for your fleet management needs has been downloaded over 300 times in the past four months by companies just like yours. Take a look and see how a simple tool like this can impact your operation."*

You'll want to have a podcast subscription sign up.

Copy idea: *"Our podcast series on Local Politics in America was the first one to achieve a subscription base of 100K listeners. Sign up and tune in weekly for the very latest on community issues that could affect you. Free, Interactive and Informative!"*

You'll want to have a general Contact Us page too, of course.

These are just some of the lead generation vehicles you'll want to use for your site. Just be sure of two things: you ask for their email address using a double opt in process and you keep the form they need to fill out very short; maybe just name, company name and email address. Phone number and company web site would be a bonus, but that's it!

In terms of how these site lead generation vehicles affect the other types of web copy, think of a spider web. You want all the other online marketing materials to be tied to each other. So, they all leverage each of the other pieces and invite them to "find out more" by directing them to the newsletter, article archive or podcast series. For more details, refer to the individual chapters that discuss each of the major web copy types.

Testing Your Copy

One of the things you'll most definitely want to do is test your copy. Like site copy updates, this is one of the most underutilized tools for content improvement. In the print world, with ads, direct mail and even billboards - it's been done for decades, but it still hasn't been adopted by the majority of businesses with an online presence. With the spread of search marketing techniques over the past few years, it is showing up on the radar, which is great. Testing is a fairly complex subject with lots of moving parts, but for the sake of keeping on topic, we'll talk about the copy part of the process here.

What is copy testing? Essentially, it's the process of finding out what copy, or what headlines and feature/benefit content, makes the most impact on your target audience. Is it this: "Discover the Top 10 Ways to Lower Your Home Utility Bill!" or is it this: "Reduce your Utility Bills by 50% Within a Month – Here's How!" Well, that's a great question. You don't know until you test. Of course, some tests will come back inconclusive. But many show an 80-20 split or 70-30 split. These types of results could be reason enough to change the copy and re-test.

That brings up a good point: Re-testing. You don't want to be in a perpetual state of testing, but you should at least test enough times to start to see a 5% or even 10% response rate! If you get more than that, then you are a rock star. Testing can be a bit subjective, so see how the test goes, survey your customers or target market for real comments and then see what you want to do. You should be able to get some good, actionable feedback.

As a large corporation, what types of online copy will you be testing? Here, the order changes from what we discussed earlier, because with copy testing, you are dealing with capturing immediate interest so they will go on to the next thing. So, here are the vehicles you should work with (in order of importance) for copy testing: email, landing page, pay per click, articles, newsletter.

How do you go about testing? Using classic A/B testing is the recommended way.

___

A/B TESTING BASICS

1. First, divide/proportion your traffic, 50/50, 90/10, or 80/20. Note: you can split them randomly, by time of day or by source (Google prospects in Group A and Yahoo prospects in Group B).

2. Decide on test stability. What does this mean? If a visitor leaves your site and then comes back, do they see the same test? Choices would be "no" stability, "session" stability, or "cookie" stability. Minimum

requirements would be session stability.

3. Last, decide what your sample size will be and set up your criteria for success.

To decide the perfect sample size, run a "null" test with your A/B test. (simply an A/A test, where you run the control against itself to determine where the convergence of results line up). You'll understand the volume of traffic you need to test when the tests converge. How do you determine success? The number of conversions or sales you receive.

To ensure the test is valid, you have to know if there's enough of a difference between the tests to declare a clear winner. Your results for the winning version should be three times larger, i.e. if A is 15, B should be 45.

Wrap Up Comments for Corporate Copywriting

To summarize, copywriting is typically viewed as *not* being very important to most corporations. There are so many examples of this online that it's pretty much a foregone conclusion. Sometimes, it's a company that's run by engineers or IT folks who think the product will sell itself – both online and offline. Sometimes it's because the value of online copy just isn't seen. Other times, it's due to the fact that smaller companies and Web 2.0 firms were the first to embrace search marketing a few years ago and saw the value first, so they got a big head start. Corporations by the dozen have ceded or are in the process of ceding to the smaller, more nimble companies. My word to the corporations is this: you'd better do something now, because if you think the web is big now, just wait a few years. It's going to be absolutely massive. When all human history is recorded, the web is going to go down as one of the biggest events of the homosapien species!

If you are a corporation that has challenges with their online content, start with the basics, read through this chapter again and see where you can start. Not everyone is going to be ready to tackle it all, but beginning is the hardest part. The best thing to do is to just pick a place and see what you can do. If you're looking for advice on this one, then start with keywords and your competitor's sites. The free stuff can also be the easy stuff. Of course, an extensive keyword analysis effort isn't free, but you'll get to that in time.

Go for it – start making all your online entities *content rich* and build even greater wealth today!

CHAPTER REVIEW

- Keyword research is a long, cumbersome process for most corporations, but doing it right can bring in big revenue.

- Ensure there is copy consistency on all your global sites.

- Getting your IT and Marketing Departments to agree can be challenging – bridge the gap with good communication.

- Watch out for the small company out-writing you and taking away online market share in the process! It happens every day.

- Don't use "Corporate Speak" in your copy.

- Find out what copy works best by A/B testing it.

CHAPTER 14

SEO COPYWRITING CASE STUDIES

The Case for Case Studies

Whenever I am trying to find out something new or learn a little bit about a company, new idea or new way of doing something, I always look for case studies. What is it they always say? If you want to be successful, take a look at who is doing it right, model them and implement a similar strategy. If you do, you'll be successful too. Well, after trying this out in real life many times (including starting my copywriting business) and seeing that it works, I am a devout believer. Reading a case study is a good way of seeing how it could be done, if wrapped around a solid process. Of course, case studies are also good choices for web content themselves, as we have discussed in other parts of this book. Almost any business can capitalize on this little tool and make a positive impact on their business.

Provada Insurance

Provada is a premier financial services company in the bay area that specializes in insurance, life settlements and other financial products and services. What they wanted to do was a very typical project for us: they were coming out with a totally new website and wanted all new copy to reflect the fresh and new offering, build out new content where appropriate and connect with their target audience more. Although keywords were important in this project, as they are for 90% of our engagements, their goal with the project was to impact online conversions to a greater extent. They wanted insurance agents, who were a big part of their customer base, to contact them for more information and to basically see how their services could improve the lives of insurance agents everywhere.

We worked closely with Provada on the different rounds of copy drafts because the choice of words was very important to them. And we wanted to get it right! Although we rarely go more than three revision cycles with any client, we went four with Provada. The message was specific and needed to be communicated in a certain way.

Project Needs

Provada really wanted to communicate how they were different. The financial services industry and insurance in general, is a very competitive arena. Standing out is tough. The great thing about Provada was that they had something that many didn't – a very long history. Roots of the company had gone back over 50 years. There may be nothing more important than stability and security in the financial services industry. They definitely had it. We just needed to communicate this, among other things to make a big impact.

We were pretty much starting from scratch with the new copy. But, having the old content there was a great starting point. We were able to see how they were communicating and where the holes were. The new pages they wanted were:

- Why Provada?
- Our 15 Point Promise
- Affiliates and Partners
- Insurance Brokerage
- Underwriting
- Life Settlements
- Agency Outsourcing
- Marketing
- Tools

The overall goal was to show all the ways that they were there to be an extension of an insurance agent's business. They wanted to show how an agent could get back to selling insurance and other financial products as well as managing relationships when they partnered with Provada.

Our Recommendations

As far as advice was concerned, we had some here and there, but for the most part, we followed the project spec. On many of the pages, there were more than the standard 300-400 words. There were many sub headers, lots of information and feature/benefit copy. The reason for this was due to the type of person who would be reading the content. These were successful insurance agents. Making the decision to partner with another, larger, entity was a big decision that took time to make. They didn't make the decision quickly and looked at a few different providers, similar to Provada to see what the choices were.

As such, these prospective clients took the time to read the site and see just what it was that Provada could do for them. So, all of our recommendations were based around this concept. We didn't want to miss anything in the copy; we wanted to ensure that we were saying the right things. The other piece of this was the lead generation parts of the site. How would they get in contact to find out more? This was a critical piece of the overall equation. So, we placed a call to action on most of the pages that encouraged the prospects to contact Provada.

Provada Copy Examples–After our work was completed

Mortgage Resource Center

This website was one of those classic ones that wanted to go from something basic and amateurish to something very robust and nice looking. We worked on this project through one of our web designer partners, David Chapman, one of the best designers on the west coast, based in Lake Tahoe. His firm is www.webrageousstudios.com. Mortgage Resource Center[44] was all about financial education, focusing on helping everyday people understand all the nuances of choosing the right mortgage, specialty loan programs, mortgage calculators and first time home buyer information. The site had a lot of depth, but didn't look all that great.

The Home page needed the most work. They needed some content that really jumped off the page; motivated the visitor to find out more, go to the other sections, etc.

The good news about Mortgage Resource Center? The changes we made impacted their site in big ways. It was one of our true successes.

Project Needs

When we got our first look at the site's Home page, we saw the immediate need. They wanted something that would balance a nice design with compelling copy. What they had currently was a very plain page with lots of copy – too much actually, no balance to the design/copy element; the page was broken up into strange proportions. The copy was dry and not written very well – it didn't flow and didn't have any real calls to action. Finally, there were too many choices on the page. Someone who jumped on the site would have an overwhelming amount of information bombarding them, all at once.

This brings up a good point. So many sites out there try to put a ton of information on each page. It really is a matter of extremes; either the site has too little – or too much information on each page. Some sites don't even have a navigational structure to them – all the information for the entire site is on one, long scrolling Home page. Have you seen these sites? Wow, its hard to imagine people are still doing this, but they are. So, even though Mortgage Resource Center didn't have that serious of an issue, the Home page still needed to be totally re-crafted and re-written.

We started with finding out what the most important parts of the page were – what did they really want to deliver to the client? Once we found this out and got answers to a few other questions, we were ready to make some suggestions.

Our Recommendations

The first thing we recommended was a new header and sub header. The current one was "Free, Unbiased Mortgage Information" – and that was it. We changed it to:

Learn the Basics; Understand Mortgage Choices, Save Time and Money!

Underneath the old header they had a three paragraph section that talked about the site, but it wasn't needed and as mentioned above, was poorly written.

We changed this long section to a simple two sentence "entrance into the site":

Our complete mortgage guidebook provides you with the unbiased information you need to make a good decision. Take uncertainty out of the equation.

For the rest of the page, we recommended making it visually appealing and going with the "less is more" concept. So, we gave them five additional sub-headers and a short call to action, benefit-rich blurb.

Mortgage Resource Center Home Page–Before

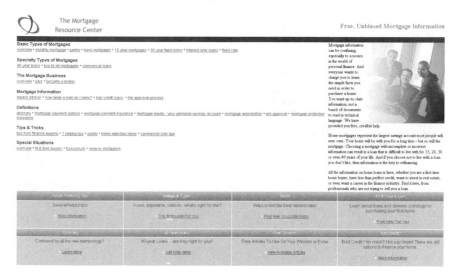

Mortgage Resource Center Home Page–After

 The Mortgage
Resource Center

Learn the Basics.
Understand your mortgage choices.
Save Time and Money!

Our complete mortgage guidebook provides you with the
unbiased information you need to made a good decision.
Take uncertainty out of the equation.

Choose The Right Mortgage

 **Is a conventional 30 year Fixed
Loan for you?**

Learn how you can pay less for your
home with a 10, 15, or 20 year loan.

MORE

Specialty Loan Programs:
Review Other Options

 Learn why Interest only and 5/1
Adjustable Rate loans have been so
popular and how you can take
advantage.

Home price above $300K? Take a
look at our advice on Jumbo Loans.

MORE

**Get Help With Challenging Mortgage
Situations**

 **Are you facing foreclosure? Are
you 3 or 4 payments behind?**

Well, life can be tough - foreclosure
happens to lots of good people.
There ARE options available Learn
more now.

First Time Home Buyer?

 Stop renting and start owning!
Your guide to everything you need to
know about living the dream of home
ownership. It's time to get in the
game.

MORE

CHAPTER 15

OUTSOURCING YOUR SEO COPYWRITING PROJECT: KEYS TO FINDING THE BEST WRITER

Hiring a great SEO copywriter can be a challenge.

There are a lot of *good* writers out there. There are even a lot of **great** writers out there. But an SEO copywriter - a great SEO copywriter, does more than just write. A great copywriter has the ability to write persuasively, research facts, and think in terms of the "total website"- because copy is only a part of the larger whole.

Many times, they see a business or idea in a new light. They draw out the key benefits of your product or service. Ultimately, a great copywriter communicates those benefits with excitement and has the ability to create that feeling in the consumer's mind.

We've all been on a website that was so incredibly compelling that it literally made us pick up the phone or email the company to order the product. Advertising brilliantly online or anywhere else, is the science and art of convincing consumers to give up their hard earned money for a particular product or service.

The Art of Persuasion

SEO Copywriters really only write for one purpose: to persuade. They increase your search engine rankings and on site conversion by persuading prospects that your product or service is better than the competition's. A great copywriter is a GREAT persuader.

The best SEO copywriters in the business are tireless researchers. Those who become the best have an insatiable interest about products, services, new ideas, consumers, the web, search marketing and advertising. Copywriters are curious people. They study human nature, your competitors, and your offering and try to find the best angle. They like to uncover new ways to represent an online product or service. They get a rush when they ultimately find the unique selling proposition for your company. A great copywriter is a GREAT researcher.

The Craft of Creation

SEO copywriters are creators. They think up compelling ideas and have the innate ability to turn them into powerful prose. Copywriters think visually. Although many people don't see them as such, they are artists too—artists of the written word. They think in terms of *words and ideas*, not numbers or logic. When coming up with the copy for a particular web page, they're simultaneously thinking of an image that will complement the copy, much like ad copywriters do. Copywriters enjoy working with other creative people, including web designers, art directors and creative directors – even web programmers in developing great websites and other online marketing pieces. A great copywriter has a GREAT ability to think in terms of the total project.

Finding the Right Angle

Sometimes trying to find the right angle for a product or service can be frustrating. A great SEO copywriter can come into a new project, quickly assess the facts, and sometimes see what others cannot. A great SEO copywriter brings a fresh perspective. They have the ability to see things in a new light. That's why a particular landing page that never generated any interest suddenly starts working like a miracle after being edited. Sometimes it's simple. Other times, it can be a little more complex. Either way, a GREAT copywriter has the ability to cast a web offering in the right light.

Copywriters focus on benefits. Great SEO copywriters find *the right set of benefits* as it relates to your offering, the industry, and your competitors and focuses on those key benefits like a laser. When a prospective customer reads the copy, they find themselves agreeing with what the copy is saying. They may have never realized they needed the product or service! That's part of the magic of it. But, the copywriter knew it. And they knew how to get inside the consumer's head. Great copywriters know people inside and out - and they know what motivates them.

Working with a GREAT SEO Copywriter

The first thing to keep in mind is that a great SEO copywriter is easy to work with. They are experienced in dealing with professionals. It helps to know what can make the difference in working with a great copywriter.

First, get your agreement in writing. A written contract is always a good idea, and can prevent difficult situations or misunderstandings from happening in the first place. A solid contract outlines the work to be performed, fees, due dates, terms and conditions.

The Money Part – Be Prepared to Make an Investment

Next, always know how much it's going to cost. Try to get your SEO copywriter to commit to a flat fee before the project begins. This way, both parties are protected. Hourly writers should be avoided. There's no incentive for them to get the job done in a timely manner. And you have no idea how many hours it's really going to take, even if they tell you up front.

Quality website copy isn't cheap. Be prepared to pay for that quality. Great copy is worth so much more than you could ever imagine, because it can literally make the difference between a product that sells five units in a month, and that same product selling five thousand units in a month. Great copywriters are worth every dollar they make.

Project Logistics – Making it Simple for Everyone

It's also a good idea to have one person- and one person only, appointed to deal with your SEO copywriter. It can be very confusing to have a whole team of people interacting with a copywriter. It can also stifle the creative process. Creating something new entails focus, patience, an easy exchange between writer and client, and giving them the space to create confidently and in original ways. If there is more than one person working with your copywriter – and worse still – trying to provide direction, conflicting ideas can arise and confusion is usually the only outcome. Designate one person to handle all communications.

Great SEO copywriters like to know exactly what they will be writing. Many times, assignments are vague. It's important to spell out in clear, simple terms, what the writer needs to know to do his best work. Sometimes the target audience is vague. Other times the features and benefits of the product are unclear. Or the web designer proves difficult to work with. In addition, a great copywriter needs to know the reason for the assignment. Is the client introducing a new product or service? Are they trying to achieve higher rankings on Google? Are they trying to convert prospects? This is a critically significant piece of the project.

Provide Materials to Work From

This is one step that sometimes goes overlooked. Many companies think if they just talk to the SEO copywriter on the phone and give the basic gist of what they're looking for, they can take the ball and run. That's rarely the case. They are coming into the project totally fresh. They may have never heard of your company. Your website may be lacking in the pertinent details. Or, you may not have a website at all. It's important to make sure you give the copywriter all the background material they need to write the SEO copy. Types of things they need are benefit statements, product sell sheets, other sites that you like, previous ads, testimonials, product brochures, market research, and information on the competitors. Having these materials makes the project so much easier for all parties.

One issue that almost goes without saying, but is also sometimes over-looked is *payment*. If you're a professional, one of the most frustrating elements of business can be issues around payment, and late payment. If you want to work with a great SEO copywriter, it's important to make this a non-issue. It's just the right thing to do – especially if you want to work with the copywriter again in the future. I've been through this many times, and it's never a fun or easy experience.

Let Them Know What You Think

Finally, give feedback. Copywriters know all about constructive criticism. It's a big part of making your website or other online marketing piece the best possible. A great copywriter will always be receptive to it. I can recall the times when I received good feedback from a client - and the times when I received not very good feedback from a client. There's a big difference, as expected. I once worked on a site for a debt relief clinic. I wrote a few pages of the site copy and a brochure. I thought the work was some of the best I had done in a while. To make a long story short, the client kept coming back with revision after revision, probably twelve in all over a period of three weeks. I finally had to let them know that we had done all we could do for them. Looking back, I don't think they really ever knew what they wanted in the first place. It didn't help that they were rude and unprofessional. Shortly after this experience, we implemented our three revisions policy. If your SEO copywriter can't get it right in three tries, they may be the wrong copywriter for the project.

A great SEO copywriter wants to know your feedback - good or bad. It's the only way to make it better. And to explode your online sales and search rankings like never before!

CHAPTER REVIEW

- Outsourcing your copywriting needs can save you time, money, and teach you some things about communicating correctly.

- Look for a copywriter who is proactive, seeks to understand your business and has a lot of satisfied clients.

- Provide the necessary materials – brochures, white papers, and completed questionnaires to your copywriter so they can write effectively for your business.

- Give specific feedback!

CHAPTER 16

SEO COPYWRITING AS A CAREER

If you are thinking about jumping into the world of SEO copywriting, you are in for a great adventure! If it is executed correctly, you could also achieve a nice level of income.

You'll Have to Write – But You'll also Have to Sell

What do I mean by that? Well, many artists, writers included, really enjoy the time they spend creating – the actual writing part. But very few like the part of going after clients, bringing in the business which is a huge part of the copywriter's life! You can't just be *willing* to do both – the writing and the lead generation – you have to be *good* at both to really make it a full time career. The hundred or so resumes from writers all over the world sitting in a manila folder in my office can attest to this very fact.

Many writers just don't like the "going after the business thing." It could be a variety of reasons: they could actually be very good at the sales piece, but they don't know how to go about it. They aren't sure what steps to take. We'll go over a few of those. It's easier than you think.

Avoid the High Maintenance Client

Once you get the sales leads, whether through your website, direct mail, emails, or referrals, you have to know which projects are going to be worth your while. I have had this situation come up many times over the past few years. I talk to the client, go back and forth a few times, ask for a deposit, it never comes, they call again, spend another hour of your time discussing additional details (all they really like to do is hear themselves talk) and you start to get a clue that this may be a "high maintenance" customer. You want to avoid them any way you can!

This situation actually happened two weeks ago with a potential client in the logistics outsourcing industry. I spent almost three hours of my time with this guy, over a few days, asked for a deposit three times, which never came, and basically decided that it was a "no win" type of project. I finally told him that I thought we weren't the right firm for his needs.

The SEO Copywriter's Typical Day

One of the best things about being a copywriter, or working for yourself, for that matter, is that there is no typical day. That's really one of the best things about the job! Let's face it, the usual 8 – 5 corporate schedule doesn't really fit the way most people work anyway, at least it doesn't for me. I do my very best work from 7am-11am and then from 8pm – 2am. Although I'm not sure why, that's when the creative juices work for me. That's when I can get in the "flow" as they say. So, typical for me might be work in the morning, run some errands in the middle of the day, go out for a nice relaxing lunch with my wife, read a little or answer emails in the later afternoon, grab a little dinner, and then go back to work right through the midnight hour.

Other people may work great from 6 am – noon and then they are done for the day. And this is probably true for many creative professions. Think about it – we are doing something that requires inspiration, to come up with something no one else has written before. That's not always easy. It *can be* if you are inspired. Sometimes you'll wake up that way, other times; you'll go all day and won't find it. Occasionally, a good batch of dark roast coffee will put me into the creative spirit.

The thing to remember is that you could do the same amount of high quality, inspired work in three hours that would take three uninspired days to match. So, that's the other thing to think about – are you the type that works in short bursts of creative explosion, or are you the type that works slow and steady, never really taking much of a break? As for me, I am the short burst type of producer. Take for example, this book. During one stretch, I wrote 60 pages in two days, I then proceeded to take a long three week break while I did some other projects before I finally got back to it. Do you know how you work? What type of schedule do you like? These are important questions because knowing the answers will help you work faster, better and more efficiently. More time for enjoying your family and going on vacation!

So, back to the original question: what's the typical day like? For me, I can do two to three small projects or one large project in a day. If it's a very large project, more like three days. But, as I'm working through the project, I almost never take more than a week to do it. I can't work on it, take a long break and get back to it a week later. If it's something I'm doing for my business, no problem, but a client typically needs it done yesterday. I probably have only 15% of my clients who plan far enough out to give me a month or more to do the project.

So, on those two to three project days, I'll work on a project for a good three hours and then take a break to answer emails, provide a quote, call clients back or pay some bills. After taking this "break," I then can get right back into the project and try to complete it. Many times, I'll take a couple of hours to do the keyword research for a project and then I'll get into it. On the one project days, I'll work for three hours take a fifteen minute break and get back into it, sometimes working through the day if the inspiration continues.

Some days will be spent doing an email marketing campaign or making calls to my large clients. I don't enjoy the phone a whole lot – so that's why I'll try to get all the calls made in one day. Even though I don't like the phone, I've been known to make sixty calls in a day – just because I knew I had to get it done and I didn't want to let it linger.

Some days, I won't work at all. I'll let the inspiration just build up and do something totally unrelated to the business. Maybe we'll go to the beach, just hang out or take a drive with my family. For us creative's, doing this can be very good for our peace of mind and energy reserves. Many of us are also introverts, so time alone can be good too.

Some of the Great Things About This Life

Probably the best thing about being a successful SEO copywriter is that you get an incredible chance to help both small and large businesses improve their operations. Many times, even for the larger companies, you're able to provide them with information on keyword phrases or their competition that they didn't have before you came on to the scene. Many companies are running very fast. They don't have time to take a look at some of the smaller details, such as website copy or online articles. They also may not have the staff to help out in this area. When you are able to help a small company, the impact is felt very quickly. Just last week, I had a client who runs an online game site email me to tell me how much easier it is for her customers to find information on the new site. She wanted to thank me for all of my hard work. Stuff like that is great and better than any recognition I've ever gotten at a "regular" job.

Another thing that's great about this career is being able to become an "expert" in your particular field. This could apply to becoming an expert in the area of SEO copywriting, or it could mean becoming a copy expert in a certain industry or group of industries. If you are the number one writer for the banking industry, guess who they are coming to almost every time? That's right – you. That can do a lot for both the ego and the pocketbook.

Plus, when you can get to a point when people are referring you by word of mouth, you save on advertising cost. As for my business, I am more of a generalist, writing content for many different industries than just a couple. I like the variety. There's another advantage – you can decide what each day will look like. You have almost total freedom to do what you want each day, but you have to be the type who is self-motivated. If working from home for yourself inspires laziness, then maybe you'd be better off getting some office space and writing there, keeping your home life separate from your work life.

Finally, there is *control.* You are driving the ship! You can build your business as big as you want, or you can keep it small if that's more your style. Chances are, if you are a writer, and/or working for yourself, you really like answering to absolutely no one. If you want to spend some money on a direct mail campaign, you can do it. If you want to work all day and night for five days and then take two weeks off, you can do it. If you want to work on a web content project on and off all day in between a workout, a child's baseball game and catching a movie, you can do it. I know that not all people like this type of thing. Although it's hard for me to believe, I know it's true. But if you are a writer, chances are, having control will really appeal to you. So, who do you answer to? Your customers. Contrary to what many people think, it's a lot easier answering to customers than it is to a boss. With customers, you have something valuable to give them that they want. In addition, there is rarely a power issue or personality conflict. Compare that to a few of the bosses you've had in the past!

Some of the Challenging Things About This Life

If all the resumes I receive every week aren't a clear enough indication, I'd have to say that the number one challenge on the list is keeping the sales pipeline full. Bringing in business can be tough, especially when you first start. I went many months writing two - three projects and bringing in $500. Even when you have had a few big months, you can then have a month that's totally dry with nothing happening. This can be a little tough trying to plan for bills and other things that come up. If you can find some level of consistency, it can become much easier.

For us, everything started to change once we were able to maintain first page rankings on Google for "website copywriter" and other keyword phrases. That's when things started getting real interesting. I can still re-member the first week I got twenty requests for proposals. I thought, wow, we've made it now! Well, that wasn't quite the case, but it sure felt good at the time, the truth is, no matter how successful you are, you always want to do more. You get inspired. You're driven. You want to bring in more income or bring on additional staff. So, keeping the business at the level you want can be a challenge.

Another challenge can come in the way of a difficult customer. I have had the easiest $2000 projects completed in four days with almost no emails from the client. I have also had $180 projects take three weeks (on and off) with twenty five emails and ten phone calls from the client. I had one client who was totally satisfied with a project and then tried to reverse his credit card payment through Paypal. You always have clients who don't pay. Thankfully, this isn't very often. Once in a while, you have a client who isn't happy with what you've written. Even after multiple attempts, it just doesn't seem to be right for them. This is usually due to the client not really knowing what they want, or the writer not understanding the project in the first place.

But you really never know who these people are. You don't get a chance to give your customers a background check before you work with them, although I have sometimes thought it would be a good idea! I guess just trying to be a good judge of character and doing a good job of filtering your prospects is probably the best advice.

Another challenge is keeping your home life separate from your work life. At the bare minimum, you want to have your own office within your home, with your own computer, phone line and fax line. This will help you do something that's very important – focus. If you can find a way to focus in like a laser beam on your project, you can tune out almost anything, and get it done in half the time. No matter what you do, however, the distractions will still be there. Why? It's your *home*. There are other things happening in this space where you live – your wife or husband is cooking dinner, your kids are playing in the next room, neighbors are knocking on the front door asking to borrow some sugar.

This is probably one reason why early in the morning and late at night work well for me – I am almost always able to find that place of focus, but at these times, it's even easier to access. Sometimes, working from home can really end up in your favor. Your spouse could give you a great idea. You don't have to be concerned with fighting traffic. You can duck out for a quick snack in the kitchen and get back to your Home page project before the inspiration goes away. If you work this way long enough, you'll find ways to make it work.

Tricks to Help Foster the Creativity: Writer's Block will be History

Take a vacation. Don't work at all. Enjoy some nice dinners, a little wine, do something you've never done before. All of this can help the creative energy to flow once again. If you are familiar with weightlifting, you know that part of the process of building muscle includes "tricking" your muscles, by lifting different weights than normal, shocking them by doing strange numbers of sets, or by just throwing a lot at them and then letting them rest. The lesson? You need to change it up; you've got to give the activity a little rest once in a while. Of course, for some of us, this may be just common sense, but others need to be reminded.

Another thing you can do is dramatically change your routine. If you work like I do - early in the morning and late at night, try working only in the middle of the day for a change. It may throw you off enough to get the brain thinking again – just in a different way. Different enough to come up with that "breakthrough idea" you've spent four hours trying to inspire.

The other little trick is to work on five or six different projects, just a little bit of each over a three hour period. By forcing your mind to shift back and forth like this, you can make some unique things happen up there in the cerebellum. For some reason, stimulation can have interesting effects. This brings me to another thing you can try – caffeine. I know for some people, cup after cup of dark java does nothing for them; no rush, no change in behavior, absolutely nothing different. For others, like me, it can have dramatic effects. I have literally gone from dead tired, with zero inspiration and no ideas to completing two, ten page attorney websites in eight hours, with a little Starbucks inspiration in a cup!

Of course, I'm not recommending using it to stay awake, but it can help when you're in a crunch and magically make you more creative.

Going After Clients with Passion and Success

Do you have a website? If not, you need one. Tomorrow. Again, lots of creative people (especially writers for some reason) they don't like to do anything that promotes their business or look like it may be sales related.

They just like to write. But, if you're working for yourself, you soon won't be. You must do the sales thing if you want to stay in business. The good thing about a website and engaging in some search engine optimization for yourself is that you can put the sales effort into "automatic pilot." If potential customers are coming to you without you having to do any cold calls – well that's just about perfect, isn't it? I bet real sales people don't even like making cold calls.

So how do you go after clients with passion and success? The first thing you want to do is fully maximize each customer experience you have. What do I mean by that? I mean, don't leave any stone un-turned. Make sure, beyond a shadow of a doubt, that they are happy. Also, ask for more. If they want you to write a simple five page website, ask to do their press releases, articles and pay per click ads as well. If the project is over and they are ready to go on their merry way, ask for referrals to their friends, business contacts and family members. Give them a 10% referral commission.

In addition, you'll want to ask for a testimonial for the good work you've just completed. These are absolute gold to your business and can be used for years to come, in many different collateral pieces and on your website. Don't let a customer go without asking for these!

The other thing to do with each and every customer is give them *more* than they asked for. Surprise them with something. It could be a more in depth competitive profile. You could ask them who their top five competitors are when you first talk to them and then go online to do a copy analysis of those companies' websites. You could do a more comprehensive keyword analysis, on multiple pages. You could give them a free press release when they do five or more pages of web content. There are all kinds of things you can do – the important thing is that you do *something*. By going above and beyond you have done three incredible things: assisted a company with their online marketing efforts, helped your business grow and one other thing - made a customer for *life*. If you think about it, how many businesses really do this? One out of ten? Alright, maybe two out of ten. You can be one of these writers. Exceed expectations with your customers. These people are going to help put your kids through college and make you look like a superstar.

Some of the Basic Tools You Will Need

What are the most important attributes? The ability to write, a creative mind and a computer. Less important are a driven nature and a natural curiosity in people or life in general. These are the high level "tools" that you need in your tool chest. What are the other things you'll need? To be fully operational, and put yourself in the best position to succeed, I've come up with a little list of "nice to have's."

The first would be a laptop computer. Its good to have in general and its also ideal for the SEO copywriter, because then, you are truly mobile. And as I've mentioned before, you don't know when the inspiration is going to strike. Yes, you can force yourself to write, but it always takes longer and is never as good. I've looked at stuff I had written from long ago that was clearly put together during a very creative time and have been amazed that I was able to come up with something so new, so inventive. A laptop can help you have more of these moments. Plus, if you are looking for a way to get away from lots of people and you're in a crowded airport terminal, there's nothing easier than simply opening up the "book" and going to work!

Next would be a fax machine with a dedicated number. No matter how technological things get, there may always be room for the good ole fax machine. Why? There are still many people out there who are anti-computer or very computer un-savvy who seem to love the fax machine. They're all sort of stuck in 1994 before the Internet revolution. But, you can't blame them. There are still probably a few die hard typewriter fans out there too. Of course, the other advantage about fax machines is dealing with signed contracts and other documents that require a signature. It's still a lot easier to just put it in the fax machine than having to scan it and email it over.

Next would be a Brother XP-2000 printer. This thing is amazing! I went from spending $300 a year on ink to $150. Plus, it's reliable, quick and very efficient.

Software. Here are the important ones: Word, Excel, PowerPoint, Adobe's Contribute, QuickBooks, and a Customer database program – ACT or Salesforce.com or some other CRM tool. For those who don't know what Contribute is, you are in for a treat. This program gives you the ability to update your website whenever you have the need. For those of us who aren't computer literate from a techie standpoint, it's great. Why? It's easy. In terms of QuickBooks, this just helps a whole heck of a lot when it comes to organizing income and expenses, and for tax time. As far as CRM goes, I have used excel spreadsheets for a long time, but I know that some people like a little more sophistication than that.

In terms of other things you could use, I would think about acquiring a couple good filing cabinets, a big thesaurus and dictionary, lots of your favorite pens, a calculator, and an i-Pod. Music helps in the inspiration department!

Questionnaires, Proposals, Contracts, NDA's and Invoices

If you are serious about becoming a professional SEO copywriter, you're going to need to *look the part*. Your potential clients are going to ask you for lots of things. You need to be ready to deliver; otherwise the business could go to your competition. The first thing that we did was put together a nice questionnaire for our clients. At first, we were a little unclear as to what to ask. We also didn't know how it should look. I came across a great version of this when I was inquiring with vendors for some SEO work on my site, so I basically copied the format of the form. I used their questions as a starting point for coming up with my own. It took a few iterations, but we eventually got it right. We now call it our "discovery document." Asking twelve very important questions of new clients has made our work much easier.

Some clients may ask for an official proposal. These are usually the larger clients who typically have to put out an RFP (Request for Proposal) and compare what you are promising to provide with what others are proposing. Sometimes you can simply put the proposal into the body of an email; other times, you'll want to make it a little more comprehensive and have it be a stand alone document. Information to include could be a profile of your business, a review of the deliverables, detailed pricing, testimonials from other clients, a project timeline and contact information.

Once you start doing work for larger companies, you may also be asked to sign a contract for services performed or a non-disclosure agreement. These are usually just formalities, but be sure to read them, regardless. There have been times when I have needed to amend them or change some language to protect my firm. Once in a great while, you get a sneaky customer who tries to put something in the contract that is clearly not fair. Very rarely, but it does happen.

Many online companies today also ask to make all business between you and them confidential and private. If you are asked to sign a non-disclosure agreement, there's not much you can do to stop it. It's very understandable that the client would want to do it, but it also means that you can't use any stories or samples from that project on your site or in any collateral.

Invoices are critical. Without them, you just don't get paid and that's not good! If you've never used them or don't know how to put one together, don't worry too much. It really doesn't matter what it looks like – just that you use them. The important thing is to send it out (email or snail mail) either upon delivery of the first draft of copy or right after the project is done. And then follow up! If you don't receive payment within two weeks, you'll need to stay on them like a hawk or you risk not getting paid for your hard work.

Doing Good Work – Making Your Clients Shine

Working in the service industry is much different than selling a product. Your reputation and the work you do – is everything. You have the rare opportunity to dramatically help your customers' business – and make it more profitable than ever. Let's face it, you are not simply writing copy for their website – you are a true business consultant, providing sage advice and wisdom. Even if you want to remain simply a writer, you will be asked by a few clients to do more. It's like that saying – "your clients will tell you what business you are in." It's very true. For many months, I told new clients that we didn't do web design. Then I realized, you know what? Why can't we do web design? Partner with a great designer who doesn't charge a lot for their service, and then mark it up a bit. So, that's exactly what we did.

You have a very good chance of finding a few companies who really need you. They could be cash strapped, understaffed or brand new. Your expertise could give them the chance to go right into the stratosphere. You know what happens then? Your business takes off. If you use that information to sell other people, you could get a ton of new business. Like the old adage, good work breeds other good work.

If you happen to be reading this book and want to become the next big thing in SEO copywriting, be sure to let me know how this advice helped you. We want all rookie copywriters out there to have the very best possible businesses. If there's anything you want to share with me about things you did to succeed, I'd love to know.

How to Build a Copywriting Empire – The Lessons of Bob Bly

Bob Bly is a superstar in my world. As I mentioned in the Introduction, without him I may have never become a successful SEO copywriter. He did all the right things, had great timing, and provided great advice for other would-be writers and one other thing: he gave back. In addition, he never brought on other copywriters and remained a fiercely passionate writer, possessing a natural curiosity that has remained on fire for over 25 years. So how did he do it? How does anyone do it? What are some things that I have done to live the copywriters dream life? Well, keep in mind, like you, I'm still on my way there. I am still on the journey. But one thing I did is in your hands right now – I wrote a book. Natural, you would think for a copywriter, but it's funny how little time we actually have for pursuing our own projects when clients are beating down the door. It's not easy to write a book. At least, it's not easy to write a *good* book, but it sure is a great idea.

Probably the best thing you can do besides write a book (or series of books like Bob has done) is go out and speak about SEO copywriting. I have actively been doing this for the past year or so and have really enjoyed it. Start by going to local business groups and service organizations and then build from there. The amazing thing about speaking is that you have suddenly added something to your resume that most writers never do – public speaking! People always think that those who go out and speak about their topic are true experts in their field. For me, it adds a great deal of variety, the chance to meet some very nice people, the ability to share my knowledge in new ways, a great way to network and finally…extra income!

One other thing you can do is write articles on copywriting topics and then distribute them across the web; much like you would do for a

The Top Ten Questions I Am Asked By Clients

1. Have you written for this industry before?

2. How much will the project cost?

3. How fast can you get this completed?

4. Are you writing the copy or is someone else?

5. Will you perform keyword research for us?

6. Can you provide a sample of your work or do one page up front so we can see if we like your style?

7. Do you write other types of copy besides web content?

8. What ideas do you have for our site? We're not sure how to make changes.

9. Do you work on retainer?

10. Do you also do web design or know some good designers?

client. In addition, you can do pro-bono work, teach a class at a local community college, form partnerships with others, and use good mailing lists to do direct mail advertising.

CHAPTER REVIEW

- Being a copywriter is more than just writing – it's selling yourself too.

- Beware of the high maintenance client – they can turn a three day project into a three week one. Not good!

- There are positives about the copywriter's life (Personal freedom, outlet for creativity, and high incomes) and drawbacks (managing multiple projects, the potential highs/lows of income).

- Set up your office and get the basics going – website, questionnaires, proposal forms and business stationary.

- After all is written and done, make your clients look good!

CHAPTER 17

THE FUTURE OF SEO COPYWRITING: THE FUTURE IS NOW

SEO Copywriting will continue to evolve and move in new directions. It will change with the times and need to adapt to growing trends and new technologies. Those that employ it will be unrelenting in their ability to find better ways to reach an ever-growing online marketplace.

But SEO copywriting and the web aren't the only things that are evolving. Consumers and consumer behavior are changing too. As we look at the future of online writing, it's important to look at how these two dynamic forces – the web and the consumers who drive it – will interact and change together over time.

Without a doubt, the Internet has revolutionized industries. It has taken the world - and the advertising world by storm. And it has only just begun to make an impact. The Internet has become a global medium with massive potential. Fifty years ago, television was considered new media. Twenty years ago, it was cable. Today, people spend increasing amounts of time online at the expense of other media. The first evidence of this audience migration appeared in 1998 in a Forrester Research report.

The researchers asked PC users which activities they were giving up to spend more time on their computers. 75% of the respondents said they gave up television.[45]

It's these and other stats that show the massive transition of consumer behavior as we witnessed the rise of the Internet.

In the Future: Greater Interactivity

Interactive. That is the real key behind the power of the Internet in advertising. The Internet is really the only medium where we see true interactivity – so far. In addition:

- It means greater viewer involvement.
- It means users can access services according to their interests and their tastes.
- They can request and receive specialized product information, make an instant purchase, all the while saving time and expense.
- Surfing the web is an actively engaging experience, similar to reading magazines.

Consumers also have the choice to "opt-in" to receiving additional information on a particular product or service. In Seth Godin's groundbreaking book, Permission Marketing, he wrote, "By reaching out only to those individuals who have signaled an interest in learning more about a product, Permission Marketing enables companies to develop long-term relationships with customers, create trust, build brand awareness- and greatly improve the chances of making a sale." [46]

Search engine optimized website copywriting is, and will continue to be, an integral part of this entire evolution. One thing we do know: written words will always be a part of the World Wide Web. There will, without a doubt, be upcoming revolutions in bandwidth and video content – who knows - we may even have 3D Internet that projects searched subject video right into your living room! Whatever your imagination can conjure; figure it to be center stage in the future of the Internet; it will be there. Things are changing lightning fast. All we can do is hold on and change *with it*. So, how specifically will copywriting be impacted? How is it currently (today) being impacted so you can be ready to take advantage of the new stuff - both personally and for your business?

Search Changes will Dictate Copywriting Changes

Although this may sound obvious, it needs to be mentioned. We've already seen, in the past few years, how new things have impacted the search landscape. There has been something new and exciting introduced every month for the past fourteen years practically. With aggressive players like Yahoo and Google out there, the environment will continue to be a dynamic one.

In the past few years, it has been blogs, Youtube.com and all of the social media sites coming out of nowhere to stake their claim. Copywriting will never be the same because of these developments.

The use of "Tags" in the writing process, and a more casual, informal, opinionated blog writing style were the big changes here. With the advent of "universal" search which debuted last year, we are seeing further changes from a copy and content standpoint; we'll get into that in just a bit. The lesson here is in monitoring the industry forces so we can make changes to the way we communicate and write online. Stay abreast of new developments. It's not copywriting that will influence the web so much. The web *will influence copywriting* – and in a big way.

How will the Web be Different in Ten Years?

Great question. What do you think? Will it be pretty much like we know it now with a few minor tweaks here and there? Or will it be practically unrecognizable? Well, let's focus on this question: does it do everything we want it to do now? Is it satisfying our needs? Some would say yes, others would say no. My follow up question would be *how do you know?* Those of us who are older than fifteen all managed to get along without the web for the earlier part of our life. We didn't even know we would need it!

One interesting thing to ponder is the television, the last major consumer and worldwide communication revolution. Did the TV change much over a fifty year period? Not really. It has pretty much always been a box that we can watch programs on. Will the Internet be like this? Some would say yes, that most of what's in place now will remain and things will just get faster and more interactive.

One thing that many talk about is how the Internet will be integrated into everyday life, no matter what we are doing. It will just "be there" – whether we are in the kitchen making dinner or out in the backyard trimming the hedges. If we have an immediate need, whatever that may be, the ever present Internet may take our verbal request/command and fulfill that need. Whether its traffic information, ordering a dozen roses for your wife, or setting up an appointment, it will all be easier and the choices more plentiful.

But having said that… who really knows *right*? Back in the early 1980's, everyone thought BETA would be the video standard, right? We were all wrong. What about Y2K? Remember that? What happened there? The bottom line is that no one really knows, we can only hypothesize, watch the thought leaders and movers and shakers out there to see what they are saying and try to innovate on our own as well. If anything is true about the Web 2.0 World, it's that we have a generation of innovators on our hands - original thinking is a hallmark of these Web 2.0 (and beyond) personalities.

I put this section in the chapter mainly to get the thinking started. How will the coming changes on the web impact copywriting? Be prepared, because change *will happen.*

Consumer's Wants and Needs will Lead Copywriting Changes

How will consumers change? That's another great question. One thing we do know is that people continue to want more personalized and customized attention. They also want to have work done for cheaper cost. Paying less is a big draw and will definitely be a concern. Will people want the ability to find things easier on the web? That's a big yes. Many times, I still find myself frustrated that I can't find a certain thing online. Even the keyword suggestion doesn't help a lot of the time. You can bet many people are working on this right now. The copywriting that will follow will be very specific and personalized to that individual.

Another thing to be aware of are *cultural changes* that will occur and undoubtedly influence the online experience. Will there be a huge change in the cultural fabric that inspires a large group of people to return to the earth and turn their backs on technology? How will that affect the Internet? Hmmm. Or will an equally large group of people become super technology savants and demand things from the web experience that are today impossible? Will the proliferation of the English language create a mostly English Internet? Unlikely, but again – all things to think about as the craft of written online communication changes along with it.

Customer (User) Generated Content

I discussed this development in earlier chapters, but it has implications for the future of SEO copywriting too, so let's discuss it a little more. We all know what user generated content (UGC) is, since most of us interact with it every day. Websites like Amazon, Trip Advisor, Epinions, Wikipedia, You Tube and My Space all have a big UGC component. But did you know that forty eight million American adults have contributed some form of user-generated content since its inception? [47] That's a pretty amazing statistic!

As one would suspect, user generated content will continue to expand and take on new forms. People trust UGC, plain and simple. With UGC, they aren't being sold to. Wouldn't it have been cool to see a list of a hundred random reviews attached to the magazine ads that you saw fifteen years ago (or even now!) for products you were interested in? Well, that's what it's like online. You can check out the bed and breakfast website and see what the owners have to say about it – but then you can get the real story from people that have been there – unfiltered and uncensored!

Over 50% of consumers that are online are reading and using UGC in research, buying decisions and just out of plain old curiosity. In addition, they expect to be able to *create* their own content. As a copywriter, this is great, right? They do the writing for us! For those online advertisers out there, it's also a good news story. Ads on UGC sites or parts of sites offer lower costs per conversion. Your ad has more impact. Not a big surprise, right? A particular part of UGC, product reviews, increases conversion rates for retail sites as well. People like to get the whole story before they buy. This is common sense, but sometimes it goes unnoticed.

Things to be concerned with would be the obvious: there may be negative or plain wrong information out there. Who is moderating UGC? Are people spamming it? There may even be lots of old UGC sitting out there that isn't really relevant anymore. These are all important issues to consider, especially if you use UGC in your business.

Universal/Blended Search: It's All New

If you've been online lately, you've seen the impact of universal or blended search and how copywriting is being impacted as a result. What is it? Essentially, Universal search compiles results from multimedia, news and other resources and places that into a single search results page. We're not totally sure how Google assembles the rankings, but it's probably a combination of traditional SEO ranking factors and, for video content – their corresponding popularity (# of comments and # of views). Some of you out there may have already seen that traditional websites and webpages have been pushed down in the rankings across the board due to

Universal search. How do you deal with this? Get some new types of content, optimize the copy/tags and put it out there!

There also appears to be an algorithmic consideration for what's trendy at the given moment. What's hot and what's happening factor in. So, the bottom line with Universal search is that more of your content can be applicable, and indexable, to the search engines. Those corporate videos you had living on your Services page? They can now live on their own and come up independently of your site. Make sure the scripting and copywriting is optimized. Don't forget about blogs and feeds – this stuff can come up faster and easier with Universal search. Make sure you are writing these correctly too.

So, how does it play out in real life, in a real search? Well, on a recent search for "monster truck shows," I found the following on the first page of the SERP (Search Engine Results Page): video content from You Tube, a couple of sites of real companies that promote the events, content appearing on Digg.com and some news about a recent event. This is very different than what used to come up in the SERP's. Try it yourself and see what comes up.

If you are planning a marketing campaign, you'll have to plan for ensuring that all of your online mediums – site, videos, press releases, RSS, etc – are speaking the same language. The copy will need to be consistent and updated, because it now may come up in the listings. These videos, podcasts and other content will take a greater role in the overall marketing mix as well. No matter what the content – text or otherwise – it will need to be optimized.

Personalized Search

Different search results for different people, that's what personalized search is in a nutshell. Launched by Google in February 2007, it gives those who sign up for Google accounts (AdSense, Google Analytics, etc.) the opportunity to have their search history monitored. If you happen to go on certain sites more than others, the sites will go up higher on your search results the next time you search that keyword phrase.

The impact on copywriting? Not a whole lot really – just keep writing fresh, relevant content and maybe you'll benefit from some of that loyal traffic. Plus, another consideration: many people may not sign up for this type of feature, including yours truly.

However, I could be wrong. There may be some big benefits that get wrapped into personalized search that may make it very attractive. If you'll be able to find what you need more quickly and have a better overall online experience, it may become the defacto standard. With all the profiles on social networking sites like Linked In, MySpace and all the others, a lot of personalized information already exists and will continue to become a larger influence on search itself. Stay tuned!

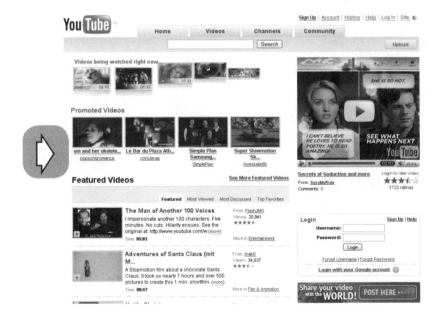

SEO Copywriting and Online Video: Video Search Optimization

It's a You Tube world, right? Well, it seems that way. Looking back, who would have thought that it would take this long for a video site to have such a major impact? Probably no one out there knew just how big it could be. Of course, most people, when they think of video, don't think of copywriting in the same thought. How are they related? Well, how about we just cut to the chase on this one?

Your videos don't stand alone. Like everything on the web, you have to think holistically. How will people find the video and where else can they be led to once they are there and have watched the video? How can you add controls to the entire experience? What you'll want to be sure to do:

1. Use target keyword infused META DATA during video encoding – this includes the title of the video, description, clip specific detail and file name.
2. Place the video on its own page with supporting copy around the video content; ensure it's relevant.
3. Use the appropriate tags underneath the video. If it's about salmon recipes, be sure to tag it as such and perhaps "fish dishes" and "cooking with seafood" as well.
4. On the page that houses your video content, use headers like "Video Site Map" and/or "News Videos" if that's what you are showing.

Just how big is online video? Consider that 7-10 billion video streams are viewed every month. Over 70% watch news video online. In a four year study, conducted by Nielson/NetRatings, they tracked a 37% increase in amount of time spent viewing content such as online videos.[48] Those numbers will continue to grow – significantly.

If you are looking for a great way to grow your content and make it richer than ever, videos are where it's at!

Social Networks Take on New Life – You are the Face Behind Your Product, Service or Brand – What Are You Writing About?

The Social Network revolution is in full force as of this writing. Driven by the younger generation and the powerful impact of sites like My Space,

FaceBook and the rest, this movement represents the merge between the web and the natural desire for people to connect in a very personal way. For businesses that embrace it, it gives power to the individual personality, branding the founder or President of whatever online company, which in turn helps support and grow the brand of the company itself. What you write on these sites, whether it be your opinion, a review, a disguised effort to promote your company – it all involves carefully crafted copy and a flair for the provocative. For some people, social networks are the first place they go, before Google, before anything else. They can truly be a home base for many people, the center of all their online activity.

How can you take advantage of this development, writing your way to influence and wealth in the near future? Dive right in. Go on to all the major sites and create profiles, start becoming an active participant and then weave in all your other online *content rich* vehicles – your blog, your podcasts, your articles – *absolutely everything* - right along with it! Through this, you can build a massive web of links from an entirely new set of sites and an entirely new group of people – friends and prospects - and then you can bring everyone along for the ride. Along the way, you'll sell a few things too, if that's what you want to do.

Remember, what you put into it equates to what you'll get out of it. Although that's very much a cliché, it's so very true with the social networking sites. Looking for places to get started? Go to YouTube, Stumble-Upon, Wikipedia, Yahoo Answers, Digg, Reddit, LinkedIn, Flickr, Del. icio.us, Facebook, MySpace, Amazon, City Search and Second Life and go to town! Start projecting your personal brand out there and writing your way to massive exposure. These are *the* hottest social media marketing sites.

The bottom line? You can and will drive new traffic to your website, blog and whatever else you want with your participation on these sites. In the future, it's going to be ten times – or a hundred times what it is right now.

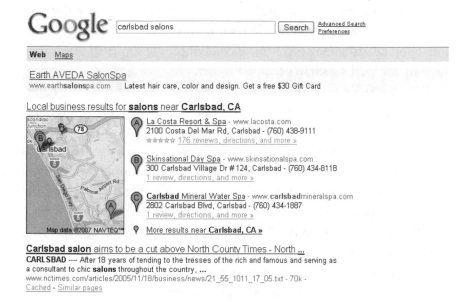

Local Search and the Implications for Copywriting

As I mentioned in previous chapters, local search is the next big thing. Of course, it's already happening, but it eventually will be a massive movement. If you are a retail business with "local only" type clients, then you are in a perfect position to capitalize on this development. Just how big are we talking about? Well, consider this: the number of general search engine users (i.e. Non –local) is only half of the online local search population. That's pretty large! Local search has been estimated at growing 20-30% annually, with over a billion searches performed every month. If you are a bank, insurance agency, auto repair facility, restaurant, salon or other serviced based business, these people are searching for you!

The thing that many local based businesses haven't grasped yet is the fact that online behavior can drive significant traffic in terms of retail walk in and phone sales. Yes, most people who surf online will tend to buy online as well if they are given the choice. But with a local business, such as a hair salon or a day spa, they need to go to the actual establishment to get the service. Local prospects will go online to find them and then go into the salon or spa later that day or that week for their appointment. What do people currently use to locate local businesses? The printed yellow and white pages are still number one. You think this is going to last? Absolutely not. If you talk to some people (me included) they're surprised that it took this long for local search to become a reality.

The big thing that hasn't happened yet (but will) is the mass movement of local businesses in setting up a web presence. Many still feel like they don't need one. Or, they are of the older generation and don't understand the web. Or, perhaps they are happy with the business they are getting and don't want to deal with more. Whatever it is, some of them will be driven out of business by those local businesses that do embrace local search. It happens in every revolution.

The implications for SEO copywriting? These local businesses will need it, that's for sure. If you have a local business, be sure to read the chapter on Copywriting for Small/Medium sized businesses. There are lots of details on the specifics for writing to the local market. You'll want to use a variety of copywriting techniques, including strong benefit statements, calls to action and language that reflects the community and people that live there. Some partnerships with other local businesses would be a good idea as well, and writing about these will show strong community loyalty.

Natural Language Queries

What if you could search more specifically and get exactly what you were searching for? Instead of using the keyword phrase "digital DVD video cameras" and getting a bunch of results that run the gamut, you could search what you really wanted in the first place: "best deals on Sony digital DVD cameras" and get exact matches in the SERP's. That would make it more efficient for everyone right?

That's exactly the vision of new search engine upstarts like Powerset, who signed an exclusive license for natural language processing technology from Xerox's Palo Alto Research Center in 2007. Could they eventually give natural language resistant Google a run for their money? Time will tell. Some people think that keyword-based search engines like Google could be challenged.

If natural search queries become the standard - or even a player, SEO copywriting will have to take into account the longer search strings.

Copywriting and Search Segmentation

If you are seeking to understand future trends, it can help to look at things from an analytical or mathematical mind as well. If you think about the search engines and the process of searching itself, you understand that there are a number of variables that are happening in terms of *segmentation*. When someone performs a search, there are lots of things that can be determined. Things like what keywords they searched, what browser they are using and what language they speak. Guess what? In the future, we are going to be able to ascertain a lot more than that. And *that* will change everything. If you know that a certain customer has been to the site before, what their buying habits are, what other sites they like, where they have searched earlier that day, etc, well then you know a lot about how to sell to that customer.

Of course, all of this will be permission based and there are privacy issues that come up too, but those will be worked through. How can search be segmented specifically? Through consumer behavior (keyword, usage, etc), how they got to their destination (PPC, natural search, social networking site, etc.), their environment (language, geographic location, etc.) and through time related factors (how recent the search was, frequency, etc.).

What about the impact on global positioning systems in hand held devices - what would happen if the search engines knew where you were at any given time. They could conceivably let you know about any retail establishment within your proximity, specials that are going on and things about the community. This would also affect copywriting on those local businesses websites in that they would want to be able to communicate to these high conversion potential prospects in proactive, call to action ways. "Come by Java Junction in the next 30 minutes and get a free extra shot of espresso in your latte," kinda thing.

Amazon.com took the lead on this a few years ago and it has worked very, very well. What I'm saying here is that in the future, this personalization and customization will take on new life. And that means massive changes for copywriting. How about individual messages written for that exact customer for that exact time, without you having to be there in an instant message or live chat dynamic? That's going to happen. Copywriting, once customer group specific, will become *uniquely customer specific.* Who said there wasn't going to be any growth in the writing field?

Consumer Reviews Continue to be Important

Opinions from your customers and potential customers will always be important. In the near future however, it's going to be more important. This great version of User Generated Content (UGC) will make the difference between an online retailer selling something – or not. If site A has product reviews by 300 customers and site B doesn't even provide the opportunity to their customers, site B will more than likely lose the sale. In terms of best practices from a copywriting and SEO perspective, be sure that your reviews can be crawled by the search engines, gives people the ability to sort the reviews by rating, and are promoted on the site, preferably the home page. Write some good sales copy where lots of people will see it, maybe something like this:

Check Out Our Product Reviews from Customers just Like You!
✳ Bixby Toy Company has a 98% Customer Approval Rating

The reality is that not everyone out there is going to *love* your product or service. It actually might be weird if everyone did. Letting negative reviews (that aren't too extreme or unfair) live and breathe helps potential customers determine if they can live with the product faults or issues. Letting these "less than stellar" reviews see the light of day can actually build trust, believe it or not.

Look, most people out there understand we live in an imperfect world; they just want to know that you accept that and aren't trying to hide anything. Let's face it; this type of feedback is actually a really great thing for any business. So, yes, in the near future, customer reviews will take on a new significance. Embrace them now! And let them do the copywriting for you!

If you are looking for places to get reviews, take a look at www.in-ods.com, www.expotv.com, www.powerreviews.com or www.bazaarvoice.com.[49]

Copywriting for Podcast and Audio Search Optimization

Podcasts have exploded in growth over the past couple of years. With 100 million plus iPods out there, it's only going to increase in number over the next several years. People who use them have discovered that they make great marketing tools, especially if they are free for the listener. Podcasts are convenient, easy and can provide a direct communication channel with your customers. You're also delivering valuable information the way the customer wants it delivered, and without commercials. Plus, you can deliver it via RSS, for free. The other great thing is that podcasts are like soap operas: your clients and prospects just keep coming back for more! They want to know what you have to say *this week*, and what the latest industry news may be. They need to stay up to date. And what's the best part? Podcasts can now be indexed by the search engines!

So how does copywriting fit into the podcast world?

Well, many of those fearless podcasters out there are doing it because they happen to be really great talkers. Let's face it, that's what you're doing when you are podcasting, you are providing information in a verbal format, like a radio talk show, without the guests.

For the talkers, they are probably fine. They may not need any help. But what about those who aren't the most gifted talkers, but still want to have a podcast? They see the tremendous value and they want a piece of it. These folks will need to write out notes, or a script to go off of. Or they may need to hire a copywriter to *write the script for them*! When they have their weekly podcast recording, they will have to be careful to paraphrase and not read the text verbatim of course.

In terms of other copywriting details, there are plenty. So let's get into it.

First, get a name for your show, one that's not in use. You'll also want names for each show/episode with a description. You'll want to develop a keyword list for the show based on those phrases that people would search for to find the show. Ensure that the audio tag parallels this. (For more nitty gritty non-copywriting SEO details on this, I recommend searching for "podcast search optimization" on Google.) In terms of what you call the podcast file name, be sure to use a unique one for each. Something like "FCReal081808.mp3" would be great for a Foreclosure Real Estate episode that aired on August 18, 2008.

You'll then want to have a separate landing page for your podcasts and be sure to optimize them. Write up an abstract of each episode, just a little blurb that explains what you are covering in that show, and use keywords as usual. You may even want to add a transcript of the shows. In terms of promoting your podcasts, you'll be employing all the great techniques of good SEO copywriting once again. Press Releases can be great for this, as well as information on your site with links to your podcasts. Blogs can also be great places to write about your podcasts: be sure to link here as well. Finally, make sure that the CONTENT of the podcasts themselves is RICH! Don't do a podcast show if you don't have some good stuff to say, said in a compelling manner. It has to be *driven by passion*. Good copywriting can help you get there, now and in the Podcast world of the future!

SEO Copywriting and Natural Search

We all know by now that Natural Search or Organic Search is a huge part of the online experience and that it will continue to be so. Although paid search has grown exponentially, it's not going to dominate. Natural search will just evolve right along with everything else on the web, the latest incarnation being the Universal/Blended search development that happened in 2007. There will be more competition for that coveted first page of the search results – more than ever, but with the segmentation that is going to happen, it will be easier to connect with your specific target audience.

The takeaway from the world of SEO copywriting would be that more and more content will be required, more relevant, more targeted and updated more frequently. Realize that your prospects and users will be getting smarter, the search engines will be getting smarter and likewise, the user experience – over which you have some control – will need to evolve in like terms.

SEO Copywriting and Email Marketing - Personalized Cross Media Marketing is HERE!

Email, as another of the big three Internet advertising mediums, will continue to be a huge force in the future. The thing that's happening now, to very positive effect, is that it's being packaged as a part of a larger campaign, using multiple communication methods. Think email and direct mail and personal websites all wrapped into one campaign. The direct mail is sent, the email is deployed to arrive the same day as the direct mail – and both direct the prospect to a personalized URL that speaks directly to their concerns, maybe with a video that features you talking about your product or service.

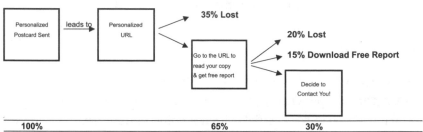

PERSONALIZED CROSS MEDIA MARKETING: SAMPLE CAMPAIGN
Taking Copy to the Next Level in a Web 3.0 World

One company that is doing exactly this is N5R.com. Companies like N5R.com are providing new and exciting email marketing solutions for hundreds of progressive companies. Their results are impressive. Consider response rates that average ten to twenty times those of traditional direct mail alone. Or campaign Network marketing referral rates as high as 40%. The bottom line is that programs they put together have produced millions of leads for clients. And it's surprisingly affordable. This means that almost anyone can now utilize this advertising medium. But it has to be done smartly, because you don't want your emails to end up in spam filters.

N5R in particular is now one of the leading direct marketing agencies in North America. They develop innovative one-to-one marketing campaigns that drive a measurable, positive ROI on behalf of their clients by driving acquisition and conversion to trial and purchase for their clients. They have developed award-winning strategies in five major industry sectors. These include Internet Marketing and Online Contests/Promotions, Permission Based Email Marketing, Text Messaging, and Success Based Email.

In Internet Marketing and Online Contests/Promotions, marketers can gather and compile behavior and preference data from prospects and customers and use this information to send targeted and relevant information. Developing ongoing programs of one-to-one communication is cost effective and measurable. Contests are the quickest and most effective way to gather this data and build relationships with customers. It's very possible to build a permission-based database of over 50,000 prospects in only six weeks, increase web site traffic by 900%, improve online sales revenue by 1,000%, and achieve $40 million in sales from leads generated by an online promotion.

With Permission Based Email Marketing, loyal clients are just an e-mail away. Where traditional marketing campaigns fail, e-mail can shine through. E-mail marketing allows companies to speak one-to-one with their audience in a respectful, intelligent and creative way. It is extremely cost-effective, provides the foundation for future marketing initiatives, and delivers measurable results.

Combined with direct mail and personalized URL's, and you have a super powerful new way to connect. Make sure you use strong copy in all!

Information Alerts

If we get to the point where the search engines know your personal preferences, could they start sending you offers and information about products and services you are interested in instead of waiting for you to search for them? This potential development would be revolutionary un to itself. It also may be an incentive for some people to provide their personal information if they know they will benefit from time and money saving information alerts. Lets wait and see on this one! It could be very interesting.

More Online Competition Across the Board

The fact that competition among businesses on the web is only going to increase almost goes without saying, but I think its too important not too bring up. Remember, things happen faster on the web, you can see what your competitors are doing almost in real time and make the necessary adjustments in your strategy or tactics to respond to their moves. Of course, you could also dictate the change too. Look, there are a lot of companies that have been studying search marketing, search engine optimization and how to improve their online writing to start accumulating their online wealth over the past few years. The only advice here is to be driven, forward thinking and customer centric. The closer you are to the consumer - and your competiton, the more educated you are on what your next move should be.

Make the moves, in content development and all other areas of your business…*today* that position you for sustained success!

The Next Step

Compared with other media, the Web is still limited in its bandwidth offerings. But it's getting better every day. With the continued improvement of bandwidth development, we will soon be positioned well to create full-featured multimedia advertising on the Internet. Once a majority of consumers have DSL capability and the computer power to access it, there will be some incredible things happening. Sites like tvtonic.com are offering some very compelling visual and audio imagery in the form of movie trailers, music videos, and other programming, including any RSS 2.0 video feed. Plus, it's all free.

Market researchers, futurists and industry experts predict that interactivity through multiple technologies and devices will change how consumers interact with marketers. Interactive advertising will soon be everywhere. So, in effect, it could be considered the age of mass customization in advertising. Advertisers will have the tools to narrow their targets and address web ads to individuals and not to a demographic or psychographic group. Why market and copywrite a commercial to one million people, most of who aren't in the target audience, when the same ad could be shown to 10,000 people who are very interested in the product or service? Some of those will even give their name and address.

Interactivity will also be a part of television. Interactive TV will be the norm in the near future, and this too is another exciting opportunity. There will be total integration between TV channels and advertisers' web sites. While we are watching TV, we will be able to interact with what we are seeing, ordering hamburgers from the McDonalds down the street or communicating with the local car dealer that we are interested in buying a car. Clicking on products we see in TV shows and ordering them will be easy. Your TV will keep track of what you are watching. Your TV will even know what kind of car you own because you'll share this information for the free oil change you're offered in exchange. "The oil change will be compliments of DirecTV, and it is only good at Jiffy Lube, which has paid to be the official oil-change provider for DirecTV." Hypothetically, that's the way it will work.

SEO Copywriting and "New Value Added" Advertising

Another major trend is what I call "New Value Added" Advertising. Let's face it; consumers are tired of advertising as usual. Many people say they hate commercials. The success of Tivo and satellite radio can attest to this. They want more from their advertising. And who could blame them? People are inundated with advertising today, every where they go. New Value Added Advertising takes the whole process one step further. Essentially, how it works is that it requires advertising to offer some incredible upfront value to the consumer before (or at the same time) a mention of a product or service offering is brought up.

For example: Kraft Foods creates a website that offers busy mothers a source for quick recipes for the family evening meal. The idea isn't to push Kraft products, but to promote Kraft as a brand that offers a service to customers. The Fresh Start orange juice ad on the next page is another great example.

There have been companies who positioned their entire marketing strategy on this tenant. Now, it will become a key part of advertising for almost everyone. Why? The consumer wants to *know you care.*

The copywriting for these pieces will need to be wrapped into the lifestyle and needs of the target market. Language about lifestyle, values,

"Value added" Print ad magazine insert from Fresh Start orange juice. They are giving the prospect a lot: recipes, a coupon, a sweepstakes entry and more!

family needs and personal tastes will all be important to bring into the writing. Benefits, of course, will be front and center.

The Future is Now!

It's important to realize that the basic tenants of current SEO web marketing and copywriting techniques will still be there in the future. But, it will look different as online commerce continues to march forward.

The future is here. SEO copywriting and online marketing will never be the same. One thing that is certain is that it will continue to be as exciting and dynamic as it has been in the past.

CHAPTER REVIEW

- The future of SEO copywriting is like the future of real estate in California in 1955 – the sky is the limit.

- Search changes will dictate the modifications in copywriting, monitor Google daily!

- Consumers will change, but human behavior will always remain consistent – people want to connect with others through the words that make up the web.

- "User Generated Content" and "Universal Search" are two new concepts that are very hot – the Future is *now*.

- Optimize your copywriting for online video and put some up on your site and around the web.

- Social Networks will be a big player in the future, as they are today, throw a few words on these sites and watch your online influence jump.

- Local Search will be a big part of the future web landscape – if you are a small retail business with only local clients – your SEO copywriting time is NOW!

- Consumer reviews will always be important – use this type of user generated copy on your site.

- Another future "thing": SEO copywriting for podcast and audio search optimization.

- Copywriting on New Value Added Advertising focuses on giving the consumer something for free *first* – before they buy from you.

CHAPTER 18

THE WRAP UP

So, here we are at the final chapter. It has been a long time coming, but we made it. If you've gotten this far then you know that we have covered a lot of material. From keyword research to blog content, from small business SEO copy ideas to copywriting for podcast and video content, we've covered it all. In fact, I'm happy to announce that no other book covers the breadth and depth of online copywriting that this one does. There is a lot of substance here, and many tools that you can start implementing right away to make a quick impact.

My goal was to give you every bit of information I could on the topic, as current as possible, and to let you know that we are only in the *infancy* of the web when it comes to search engine optimized copywriting. The way we optimize will undoubtedly change, but the importance of the online written word will remain. For the very latest, as well as information and discussion about Content Rich, the book, my seminar and speaking schedules go to www.contentrichbook.com.

 If you haven't already emailed us for your free bonus items, take a minute to do it now. (readers@contentrichbook.com)

So, how do we sum up everything that we covered in such detail? Well, I think the best way is to give you the "takeaway" bits of advice and recommendations – the points I want you to most remember as you go back to your businesses and try to make some of the copy changes I discussed. We'll make this final chapter brief and to the point – just the facts. Although all of this is repetition from previous chapters, it hasn't been assembled together like this for maximum impact. So, here, as we conclude

CONTENT RICH, *Writing Your Way to Wealth on the Web*, are the Final 15 Points:

1. **Review your Copywriting Goals**

    Is your site in need of a copywriting makeover? You may think so after reading this book. Some of you, however, (probably 10%) may be saying to yourself *"I think we are doing everything right, our copy is performing well; we are driving people to the site and converting prospects at a high rate too."* – and you would be right. Some sites out there are doing very well. Those are the ones we all learn from.

    So, what are your copywriting goals? Do you need to do a better job of driving more people to your site, turn these prospects into sales or both? Are you trying to build your brand and need some consistent and recognizable language on your site, blog, articles, press releases and other online vehicles? Perform an honest assessment of what you need to do – and be sure to ask others for their opinions too. Ask me if you like!

2. **Perform Thorough Keyword Research**

    I think the number is around 95%. What am I referring to? Having written for hundreds of companies in every major industry, on three continents I would say only 5% of the businesses out there do a thorough and complete job on keyword research. Some don't do any keyword research at all. These are the ones that can get the quickest impact. I can't stress enough how important this step is. But it's not enough to simply do the research and have in your hand a list of all the important words and phrases. The other part is using them in the right way on your sites, blogs, articles and everything else.

    One of the best things you can do is go on to WordTracker.com and KeywordDiscovery.com and sign up for a free trial. If I were you, I would do it right after finishing this book. Take the time to make a big impact today!

3. **Engage in an online copy "audit" for your site**

   Ask your ten closest friends to look at your website content. Next, ask ten of your best customers. Find out from them what they would recommend to make the site better. Most people have never ever done anything close to this! But you know what? You can find out some very interesting things from these people. Some of the feedback will be bad or incorrect – but I guarantee you'll get some high quality, actionable advice too. Look, you are too close to your site to see what it needs. Not always – but many times, this is true.

   How many times have you been on your site or blog in the past week? If you're like me, you're on there all the time. You need to back away, see it from a new perspective – from someone else's perspective! After you get the feedback, lump it together with your own personal assessment and rank what's most important. What will you start with? A series of articles that focus on topics in your industry? A new blog with fresh, inspiring content? It's different for everyone.

4. **Analyze your Competitors' Copy**

   We all need to take some lessons from the old school brick and mortar companies with this one! It seems like it's an epidemic actually – no one does any competitive copy research online anymore. Market research is a hallmark of many companies that were around before the Internet. They would study ads, do focus groups, buy expensive industry reports, etc. In the online world, we barely even go to our competitors' websites to check out what they are saying (or writing). And that's free!

   If you want to have 30 very productive minutes, working on your business, search for your keyword phrases and click on all the sites on the first two pages (Both PPC and natural listings). Read their copy, check their source code. How do you compare? Are they offering some specials? See what you can do to get a competitive advantage in the copywriting area!

5. **Go back Through the Book and Study the Charts and Areas Marked with an Arrow– These are the Critical Points**

The charts and other key areas that I included in this book were meant to get you to think, meant to provoke and help you see your business, and all the types of online copy that you can write, in a new light. I happen to think that online copywriting is really a distinct subject area that could be taught – even in a classroom setting. The areas marked with an arrow encompass the most important points in the book and if this were a class, would be the daily and weekly topics discussed during the semester. You wouldn't be able to pass the mid-term and the final test without knowing these through and through!

You may have heard of *keyword penetration* and *keyword proximity* before for example, but didn't know all the details. Points like this are too important not to read again.

6. **Review your Site (and other online "vehicles") for Potential areas of Content Development**

Do you have a blog but haven't contributed to it in two months? Develop new content! Do you have hard copy brochures that promote your business through direct mail, but don't use email copy to connect with your customers? Investigate some of the email marketing vendors out there like Vertical Response and Constant Contact and see how you can integrate this copy technique.

7. **Build Out Your Content**

This is the writing part! After you've done all of the above, have some ideas and have written up an outline or rough draft, get out the keyboard and start putting words to paper. It may take you a few drafts to get it right. It will also take some time, if you have lots to do, it could be a two to three month project. Writing isn't always easy, but online, it will pay huge dividends, the biggest dividends ever actually. Much better than direct mail could ever do for you.

If you are looking for ways to get inspired or just can't seem to get anything down – then it's time to consider hiring a copywriter to do it for you. Don't struggle with it. If it's not your strong suit, then you may save yourself a lot of time and even more aggravation if you just let a pro do it.

8. **Social Media Sites – Set Up Profiles and Start Participating with New Content**

For the savvy Web 2.0 youngsters out there, this step has already been completed, no doubt. They set these sites up after all! But for most of us, we just don't get it. How can participating on FaceBook or LinkedIn help my business? Let me give you some sound advice: don't even think twice about it… you need to just jump on these sites and get involved. You won't regret it.

Ways to Improve Your SEO Copywriting

1. Practice

2. Take a writing class – hands on training

3. Study great SEO content

4. Analyze your competitors' copy

5. Write and then ask for feedback from others

6. Try different ways of saying the same thing and test it

7. Stop talking and start writing!

8. Brainstorm!

9. Do something else creative for inspiration

10. Find out what your "best" time of day is and write then

Why? People are getting business from being affiliated with them. That's all you need to tell me! I'm in!

9. **Podcasts and Video Content – What Could you Do in These New Areas?**

    This is where it gets exciting! How cool that we can now connect with prospects and others with audio and video. This is much more than any pre-Internet CEO ever had a chance to use to stroke his or her ego! Just think about it – you could be practically everywhere and anywhere people go online to get your message out. The viral potential is massive. After you're retired in ten years, you'll thank me for this one.

    Write those scripts, tag the content, build out your pages with optimized copy and start taking advantage today.

10. **Get Your Content Out There!**

    Promote, Promote, Promote! Leverage your content across all online vehicles – blogs, affiliate sites, social media sites, the search engines – do it all. Use the content ten different ways in ten different online "channels." When you write high quality, optimized copy, you can get *lots* of bang for the buck.

11. **Tweak Your Content and Regularly Add to It**

    Web copywriting, like anything online, is an on-going activity. It never stops. It's a living, breathing, interactive, growing thing. It's alive! So, you'll need to continue to add to your blog, build out your articles, submit press releases and add pages to your site. Make it something you want to do. If you are passionate for your business, it will be something you enjoy. If not, then maybe you aren't in the right business!

    One note on this one: maximize user generated content (UGC) too! Let others write content for you. This is one of the smartest things you could do.

12. **Analyze Your Web Analytics with WebTrends or ClickTracks**

    You never really know what's going on with your content

unless you measure and analyze it. That's truer for the web than anything that came before it, because almost *everything* can be measured on the web. Do you have a web analytics program? Do you look at it? Perhaps you have some analytics capability with whoever hosts your site. I know Yahoo and Google both offer this, as well as many of the larger hosting providers.

You'll want to know which pages on your site get seen the most and where people go on your site. What copy is making the biggest impact? At what point are they being converted to a sale? Study the data.

13. Monetize your Content and Focus on Building Customer Relationships with Your SEO Copy

If you have a blog, maybe you have enough people coming to it to start advertising. If so, this is an exciting time! That's one of the best ways to make money online. You're making money while you sleep! Not bad.

Speaking of advertising, you could sell ad spots on your newsletter and website as well – but you have to build up a large database for your newsletter and a big, steady stream of new traffic to your website first. How do you do that? Follow the advice in this book and do some additional SEO on your site…that's the first step. Next, build your brand. Easier said than done, but copywriting will be a big part of the equation.

14. The "Content Rich Quotient" (CRQ)

Remember the Content Rich Quotient from the 1st chapter? As you may recall, this is a measurement tool that helps you understand where you are along the path of your online copywriting evolution. The four key areas of the CRQ were:

- **Content Breadth Factor:** This analytic places importance on how many types of web content you are utilizing and how qualitative they are in terms of user benefit and SEO factors. What are the types of content we are referring to? Website, Article, Press Release, Blog, Pay Per Click and Newsletters.

- **Social Media Optimization (SMO)/Search Engine Optimization (SEO) Balance:** As I discussed, SMO focuses on making changes to optimize a site so that it is more easily linked to, more highly visible in social media searches on custom search engines and more frequently included in relevant posts on blogs, podcasts and vlogs. SEO, the practice of using a variety of techniques to improve a site's ranking on the search engines is the other factor. By doing both of these things well, you are helping to build rich content.

- **Content Effectiveness Measurement:** Analyze peoples path through your site. Where are they just before they go to the order page or contact page? Which content is making the most impact?

- **The Content "Clincher":** Which specific language/copy is truly responsible for the sale (or conversion)? If online content converted a prospect, you want to know which exact words, feature/benefit statements or specials made them say YES.

Get a fix on your CRQ! It helps you understand your content strengths and weaknesses.

15. **Read this Book Again, Check out our Blog – www.contentrichbook.com and look for Future Editions!**
    Both the blog and the book will be updated frequently. Be sure to check regularly!

16. **Contact Me Directly with Your Questions!**
    Jon@ContentRichBook.com

Final Thoughts

As we come to a close, just want to leave you with two final thoughts:

Make your prospective customers feel like they are buying from a friend.

Your goal through strong copy is to build relationships and attain more sales – that's a given. But you also want to reduce your customer acquisition costs, improve your customer loyalty rate, and overall, increase each customer's lifetime value. In addition, you want to learn something from them – you want this to be a true relationship – even a *partnership,* with their user generated content, etc. Let's face it, these people are going to be helping to **define your brand** – yeah, that's right: *define* your brand, not just *buy* from you.

Leverage content created in one online vehicle/silo into the all the other silos.

Example: create a topic and post it on your blog, send it out via email and RSS and allow prospects to respond to it. This builds community around your offering, providing a forum for feedback, interaction and yes – sales. What you learn can be posted on a "Knowledge Wiki." Think in terms of your "online copywriting universe" – how all of your seo copy vehicles interact, effect and support each other.

If there's one thing that almost **all** businesses miss, it's this one. They'll write some articles and distribute them out, but not use the ideas expressed in the articles for blog content or for their newsletters. Save time! Maximize the value of your copy! Get the most out of it that you possibly can; you'll increase the viral nature of your content and bring more people to your sites and blogs.

So, that's a wrap! You've completed the book, and have come away with some great information, but the real work is just beginning! Now is the time to put some of this stuff into practice. So, dust off that laptop and start coming up with some ideas. How can you grow your web presence through the written word? How do you ensure that its search engine optimized? How can you differentiate your site or blog from your competitor's so you really stand out? What can you write *today* to make an impact tomorrow?

As I bid you a fond...*written*...farewell, please know that I would love to meet you in person, or at least via email. The *Content Rich* book tour may be coming to a town near you soon! In addition, I may be speaking on the topic in a hotel lobby or corporate boardroom in your city too. I'd love to have you join us; there's nothing quite like face to face learning. Plus, we have a lot of fun at our events.

May your websites do well, may your businesses be successful and may the rich content that you build put you well on your way to web wealth!

Thanks for reading!

Resources

Appendix

SEO Copywriting Tools

Link Popularity: www.linkpopularity.com

Marketleap Free Tools: http://www.marketleap.com/services/
freetools/default.htm

NetMechanic Code Checker: http://www.marketleap.com/services/
freetools/default.htm

Report a Google Spammer: http://www.google.com/contact/
spamreport.html

SEOTool Set: http://www.webuildpages.com/tools/default.htm

Plagiarized copy search: http://www.copyscape.com/

Traffic rank: www.alexa.com

SEO report: http://www.urltrends.com/

Web page analyzer: http://www.websiteoptimization.com/services/
analyze/

Search Engine Spider Simulator: http://tools.summitmedia.co.uk/
spider/

Go Ranks SEO Tools: http://www.gorank.com/seotools/

SEO Book Tools: http://tools.seobook.com/

SEO Copywriting Blogs

Content Rich! www.contentrichbook.com

Keyword Research Sites

WordTracker: www.wordtracker.com

KeywordDiscovery: www.keyworddiscovery.com

Nichebot: http://www.nichebot.com/

Top 10 sites for a keyword: http://www.webuildpages.com/cool-
seo-tool/

SpyFu: http://www.spyfu.com/

Seodigger: http://www.seodigger.com/

Keyword Difficulty: http://www.webuildpages.com/tools/default.
htm

Keyword Identifier: http://www.googlerankings.com/ultimate_seo_tool.php

Keyword density measurement: http://www.live-keyword-analysis.com/

Search Engine Keyword Verification Tool: http://www.marketleap.com/verify/default.htm

Key Compete (Keywords Your Competitors are Buying): www.keycompete.com

Trellian Competitive Intelligence: http://ci.trellian.com/

Help with Writing Sites (Grammar, Style, etc)

Dictionary: http://dictionary.reference.com/

Thesaurus: http://thesaurus.reference.com/

The Purdue Online Writing Lab: http://owl.english.purdue.edu/

Business Writers Free Library: http://www.managementhelp.org/commskls/cmm_writ.htm

Brief Guide to Business Writing: http://www.biz.uiowa.edu/faculty/kbrown/writing.html

Bulls Eye Business Writing Tips: http://www.basic-learning.com/wbwt/

Suite 101: www.suite101.com

SEO Books

SEO Book: www.seobook.com

Search Engine Marketing, Inc – Mike Moran and Bill Hunt

Style Guides/Usability/Design

Jakob Nielsen's Use It: www.useit.com/papers/webwriting

Web Pages that Suck: http://webpagesthatsuck.com

Edit Work: www.edit-work.com

A List Apart: www.alistapart.com

W3: www.w3.org/provide/style/overview.html

Web Analytics

Clicktracks: www.clicktracks.com
Web Trends: www.webtrends.com
Google Analytics: http://www.google.com/analytics/
Mint: www.haveamint.com
Competing Websites Traffic Trends: http://www.compete.com/

Press Release Sites

PR Web: www.prweb.com
PR Newswire: www.prnewswire.com
Business Wire: www.businesswire.com
Marketwire: www.marketwire.com
Primenewswire: www.primenewswire.com

Social Media Sites

Linked In: www.linkedin.com
Facebook: www.facebook.com
Flickr: www.flickr.com
Digg: www.digg.com
YouTube: www.youtube.com
Del.icio.us (social media bookmarks): http://del.icio.us/

Blog Related Sites

Blogger: www.blogger.com
Typepad: www.typepad.com
Wordpress: www.wordpress.org
Bloglines: www.bloglines.com
Live Journal: www.livejournal.com
Technorati (blog ratings): www.technorati.com

Pay Per Click Advertising

Google AdWords: http://adwords.google.com/select/Login
Yahoo Search Marketing: http://searchmarketing.yahoo.com

Email Marketing Vendors

Constant Contact: www.constantcontact.com
Vertical Response: www.verticalresponse.com
Yes Mail: www.yesmail.com

Article Distribution Sites

Article Marketer: www.articlemarketer.com
The Phantom Writers: http://thephantomwriters.com/index.php
Article Announce: http://www.all-in-one-business.com/groups/
Directory of Article Directories: http://www.arcanaweb.com/resources/article-directories.html
Netpreneurnow: http://www.netpreneurnow.com/internet-marketing-articles/
Idea Marketers: http://www.ideamarketers.com/library/signup.cfm
Go Articles: http://www.goarticles.com/
Article City: http://www.articlecity.com/article_submission.shtml
All Freelance: http://www.allfreelance.com/submitarticle.html
EZine Articles: http://www.ezinearticles.com/

Events

Search Engine Strategies: www.searchenginestrategies.com
Pubcon; www.pubcon.com
Ad:Tech; www.ad-tech.com
Emetrics Marketing Summit: http://www.emetrics.org/

Publications

Search Marketing Standard: http://www.searchmarketingstandard.com/

B to B Magazine: http://www.btobonline.com/

Website Magazine: http://www.websitemagazine.com/

Professional Organizations

SEMPO: http://www.sempo.org/home

eMarketing Association: http://www.emarketingassociation.com/

International Internet Marketing Association: http://www.iimaonline.org/

SeoPros: http://www.seopros.org/

American Marketing Association: www.marketingpower.com

Direct Marketing Association: http://www.the-dma.org/index.php

News and Information Resources

Marketing Sherpa: www.marketingsherpa.com

Wikipedia: www.wikipedia.org

ClickZ: www.clickz.com

Top SEO's: www.topseos.com

Internet Marketing Index: http://www.internetmarketingindex.com/

EMarketer: http://www.emarketer.com/

SEO Chat: www.seochat.com

Google SEO Info Page: http://www.google.com/support/webmasters/bin/answer.py?answer=35291

Google Webmaster Information Page: http://www.google.com/webmasters/index.html

Google Hot Trends: http://www.google.com/trends

Indicateur.com: http://google.indicateur.biz/

Internet Search Engine Database: http://www.isedb.com/

Media Post: http://www.mediapost.com/

Pay Per Click Analyst: http://www.payperclickanalyst.com/

Search Engine Blog: www.searchengineblog.com
Search Engine Dictionary: http://www.searchenginedictionary.com/
Search Engine Guide: http://www.searchengineguide.com/
Search Engine Watch: www.searchenginewatch.com
Search Engine Journal: http://www.searchenginejournal.com/
Search Engine World: www.searchengineworld.com
Yahoo! Buzz Index: http://buzz.yahoo.com/
Webpronews: www.webpronews.com
Site Pro News: www.sitepronews.com
Search engine forums: http://www.searchengineforums.com/
Internet Marketing Research: http://www.umassd.edu/market-research/

Discussion Forums

High Rankings Search Engine Optimization Forum:
http://www.highrankings.com/forum/
SEO Rountable: http://www.seroundtable.com/

Recommended Small Business Websites

Maria Marsala: www.coachmaria.com
Marketing Knowledge Source: http://www.knowthis.com/
SCORE: http://www.score.org/index.html
Inc: http://www.inc.com/

SEO/General Marketing Blogs - Info

SEO Moz: www.seomoz.org
Marketing Pilgrim: http://www.marketingpilgrim.com/
Mike Grehan: http://www.mikegrehan.com/
Traffick: http://www.traffick.com/
Future Now: www.grokdotcom.com
Marketing Profs: http://www.marketingprofs.com/
IMedia: http://www.imediaconnection.com/

Sites/Blogs for Copywriters

AWAI: http://www.awaionline.com/
Quotes: http://www.quoteland.com/
Freelance Writing Jobs: http://www.freelancewritinggigs.com/
The Renegade Writer: http://therenegadewriter.com/
Web Writing Info: http://www.webwritinginfo.com/
The Golden Pencil: http://www.thegoldenpencil.com/
Copywriters Underground: http://www.copywriterunderground.com/

Search Marketing Firms

Lead to Conversion: www.leadtoconversion.com
Intrapromote: www.intrapromote.com
Rock Coast Media: www.rockcoastmedia.com
Net Advantage: www.netadvantage.com
Web Search Engineer: www.websearchengineer.com

Podcast Help

ITunes Podcasting: http://www.apple.com/itunes/store/podcasts.html
Podcasting News: www.podcastingnews.com
Podcast Alley: http://www.podcastalley.com/

Online Video Help

You Tube Video Toolbox: www.youtube.com/video_toolbox

End Notes

1.Bob Blys Copywriters Handbook
2. Maria Marsala
3. B to B Magazine 11/12/07 Hollis Thomases
4. Search Engine Strategies
5. PR Web
6. Skype
7. Sunset Wine Club
8. Cameron Hughes Wine Club
9. You Tube
10. MarketingSherpas Ecommerce Benchmark Guide 2006
11-15 Search Marketing Fact Pack 2006 - Ad Age
16 6SMarketing.com / Zephoria.com
17 Jakob Nielsen www.useit.com 2007
18 Keyword Discovery / Wordtracker
19 Spy Fu, SeoDigger, the SEO Book Keyword Tool
20 Web Trends / ClickTracks
21 Crowley Marine
22 Best Places in Hawaii.com
23 Catchquick.com
24 Joe Sugarman
25 Ginsu Knives
26 Site Pro News
27 Web Pro News
28 Link Popularity
29 findarticles.com, goarticles.com, articlecity.com
30 yourvirtualresource.com, businessevolved.com, echievements.com
31 Jill Whalen of High Rankings
32 Article Marketer.com
33 PR Newswire, PRWeb, Business Wire, Marketwire and PrimeNewswire
34 press-world.com, inthepress.ru, free-press-release.com
35 blogger.com, typepad.com, wordpress.org, bloglines.com, livejournal.com, technorati.com
36 Flickr.com
37 Digg.com
38 Technorati's State of the Blogosphere Report - April, 2007
39 Wikipedia
40 Constant Contact, Vertical Response, Yes Mail
41 Jupiter Research 2007
42 Zappos.com
43 Oakwood.com
44 Webrageous Studios/Mortgage Resource Center - David Chapman
45 Forrester Research - 1998
46 Seth Godin, Permission Marketing
47 ClickZ - 5/30/06
48 Nielsen/Net Ratings Study 2007
49 nods.com, expotv.com, powerreviews.com, bazaarvoice.com

Index

QUICK ORDER FORM

Email Orders: orders@encorepublishers.com
Telephone Orders: (760) 451-8700
Fax Orders: (760) 451-8670. Send this form.
Postal Orders: Encore Publishing,
                     124 S. Mercedes Road,
                     Fallbrook, CA 92028

Please indicate which item you are purchasing and the quantity:

Content Rich: Writing Your Way to Wealth on the Web

Hardcover Book	$19.95	Quantity	___
Audio Book	$29.95	Quantity	___
E-Book	$14.95	Quantity	___
Content Rich LIVE!	$79.95	Quantity	___

Please send more information on:

❏   Speaking / Seminars

❏   Consulting

Name: _____

Address: _____

City: _____ State: _____ Zip: _____

Telephone: _____

Email Address: _____

Website URL: _____

Sales tax: Please add 7.75% for products shipped to California addresses

Shipping by Air:
U.S: $4.00 for first book and $2.00 for each additional product
International: $9.00 for first book and $5.00 for each additional product (estimate)

QUICK ORDER FORM